WHAT OTHERS ARE SAYING ABOUT THIS BOOK

"Winning is the result of passionate action. This book shows you how. Buy it!

—Bill Cates, speaker and author of *Get More Referrals Now*

"This book inspired me to seek ways out of my comfort zone. When I read the book, I was looking for a way to shake things up in my life, and it provided a concrete approach and road map for doing so. I can't wait to see where it takes me!"

—Lori Wilson, manager at Micros, Inc.

"This book is a gold mine, rich with tools and resources that can help both coaches and clients generate dramatic (possibly transformative) changes."

—Celia Blalock, Director of Organizational Learning and Performance, AARP

"Doug's book puts him at the top of the list when it comes to personal and business coaches. A must read!"

—Tim Connor, speaker and author of 60 books including the bestseller *Soft Sell*

"Life requires passionate action and Doug Gray is the perfect guide."

—Dawn Billings, author of *Greatness and Children*, and *America's Journey Back to Greatness*

"This book is a wake-up call for those of us who are missing the adventure of life. Doug Gray has done a masterful job of blending personal experience and the experience of others. His book offers exciting and insightful ways that all of us can use. His use of models and case studies make the adventure model of personal development come to life."
—Leo McAvoy, PhD, Professor, School of Kinesiology, University of Minnesota

"This book is an exciting and sure-footed process of discovery that quickens the heart and enlivens the mind. Doug Gray has done something that few do this well – inform, educate, and inspire with many practical exercises and case studies. It was a galloping pace from page one, bringing forth the best in me."
—Lloyd Raines, executive coach at Georgetown University and Principal of Integral Focus

"Has life lost its zing? Rediscover the adventure in your life through Gray's book. Motivating and practical, it will help you move ahead with positive life changes with an adventurous spirit."
—Kathy Conron, executive coach at Nextel

"Winning is the result of passionate action. I encourage you to buy this book."
—Linda Blackman, speaker and coauthor of *The Sales Coach*

"This book offers simple, easy to use tools; tools that are essential for living the meaningful life. If you want adventure, run, don't walk, to the nearest bookstore."
—David Cockrell, personal coach and therapist

"This is a useful, practical book for anyone who needs to get unstuck and overcome the challenges in life."
—Paula Basile, Organizational Development and Training, University of Maryland

"This book is everyone's fantasy with some realistic steps on how to achieve it. Many people at my stage of life want to try adventures, but are afraid to start. This book helps kick start the process!"
—Susie Rosenbaum, Middle School Head, Norwood School

"This book will help make your life more of an adventure. Get the message and get moving!"
—Michael Angelo Caruso, author of the 5 Cool Ideas series

PASSIONATE ACTION

*5 Steps to Creating
Extraordinary Success
in Life and Work*

DOUG GRAY

GRAY PUBLICATIONS
HUNTERSVILLE, NORTH CAROLINA

Library of Congress Control Number: 2007902811

ISBN-10: 0-9758841-5-8
ISBN-13: 978-0-9758841-5-7

For bulk sales contact www.action-learning.com.

Published by Gray Publications.
9441 Titus Lane, Huntersville, NC 28078

TABLE OF CONTENTS

ACKNOWLEDGMENTS PLUS

Throughout this book, I have cited the colleagues and sources that have influenced me. Citation details are in the Recommended Reading section.

Scores of people have contributed to this book. Many thanks to those editors and colleagues including Joe Amato, Kim Archer, Paula Basile, Laura Burch, Stephanie Burgevin, Celia Blalock, Trey Cassidy, Bill Cates, David Cockrell, Cathy Conron, Lorie Falk, Shelley Fox, Dan Goodman, Patti Harden, Mary Beth Hatem, Diane Hetherington, Krista Kurth, PhD, Pam Leigh, Don Mann, Leo McAvoy, PhD, Peter Meredith, Ken Norton, Lloyd Raines, Susie Rosenbaum, Chris Rumohr, Suzanne Schmidt, PhD, Ken Smith, Rosalynn Whitehead and Lori Wilson. My wife and children deserve my most sincere thanks and love. Without their support this book would not exist.

The purpose of this book is to educate and entertain. My sincere hope is that after reading this, you will experience action-based success. This guidebook is a tool, like a map or a compass. Use it and share it.

This book is dedicated to you, each reader, with the hope that you have extraordinary success in your life and work.

CHAPTER 1

Your Passionate Action

■ PASSIONATE ACTION EXAMPLE #1

It was about 3:00 a.m. and 25 degrees. During this adventure race, we had already bicycled, paddled, run, and walked over 180 miles. Our team had started racing at midnight the night before; we had been pushing it for over 27 hours. Brian and I had finished the race last year, and this year we thought we should race as a team of four. So, we talked Bill and Laura into joining us. Bill preferred shorter races. Laura had the personality of a tireless cheerleader. I was the team captain, lead navigator, the coach, the climbing and paddling instructor, supposed to be an expert on team building, expected to be the first one down the rappel. Now I was tired and scared.

We had not slept in two days. We had been slightly lost, then navigated our way up and down the steepest terrain in the country, every corner of the New River Gorge in West Virginia. Now we stood on the edge of the cliff, with thick dew clouds from the New River 1000 feet below us. I was expected to rappel 200 feet down, then hold the rope for my teammates, so they could safely descend. I looked down into the clouds. They were as thick as

mashed potatoes, harsh and cold in the yellow-white moonlight.
I didn't want to do it.

Tired. Cold. Scared. The next team was 18 minutes ahead,
and I knew I should just suck it up and get over the edge. We had
a good chance of catching them, if only I could get my feet to
move. The climbing guide said that there was a camp fire down
below. Warmth. Comfort. A place to rest. My teammates said,
"It's time to go. We can't miss you 'til you're gone. So get going!"

YOUR PASSIONATE ACTION

You may be on a similar edge, due to inspiration or necessity.
You are seeking passionate action in work or your personal life
or both. You may feel that you are about to drop into a dark,
unfamiliar place. It may seem cold and scary. But, there may also
be camp fires along the way.

Thankfully, you are not alone. You may have friends and family, a support team, encouraging you to take your first steps. You
may have a supervisor telling you that you need to do something
different. You may have loved ones telling you that you can do
something more in life. These are the external forces pushing
you into action. Whether you feel excited or afraid or some other
emotion, this book is for you. It is like a climbing rope; it con-
nects you to a strong anchor, safely tied to the earth.

Internally, you may also have a call for passionate action.
Something undefined, magnetic, stronger than gravity, may be
pulling at you, forcing you to take steps away from the familiar.
Your face in the mirror may have suddenly become unfamiliar.
That internal force may be carrying you away from old results
and patterns. The scheduled challenges in your day timer or palm
pilot may no longer excite you. Perhaps you have had an illness
or accident or loss that has shocked you. Regardless, now you

suspect that there is another way to be. And it has something to do with stepping into a life of not just action, but a life filled with passionate action.

It doesn't have to be outwardly dramatic. You do not need to leap from a cliff or raft the Colorado River. You do not necessarily need to quit your day job or vow to get married. Unless one of those steps helps you move to the next level, your steps toward passionate action can be taken quite close to home.

Your steps may include saying "No" when you want to, calling five "long-lost friends" each day for a week, sleeping on the other side of the bed, inviting a challenging person to lunch, or changing the way you interact with a difficult person. You will define your steps. The character of your next steps may be internal, private, subtle, or profound. The domain of your next steps may be physical, emotional, cognitive, spiritual, financial, social, or something else. This book provides a proven model, the five steps of the Passionate Action Model. In whatever way this book calls you, it will lead to change.

DEFINITIONS

Here are three simple definitions. You are "passionate" when you are capable of or are expressing feeling. The word passionate is stronger than related feelings like enthusiasm; it is unique to each of us, dependent upon your individual values, and connotes strong emotional energy. "Action" is defined as what you say or do. "Passionate action" is defined as a state of being that leads from your strongest feelings to constructive action. Passionate action is a process with five steps that you can develop and learn. This book will help you do so. Passionate action occurs when you are fully engaged, fulfilled, and capable of winning. The result can be extraordinary success in your life and work.

■ PASSIONATE ACTION EXAMPLE #2

One of my coaching clients, Jeff, is a senior manager in a financial services company. His story is representative of hundreds of people in hundreds of professions. Perhaps even yourself.

Jeff's department, and his company, needs to upgrade almost every quarter. Every day brings external threats from hungry new upstart companies who want to steal customers and market share. Internally, there are hundreds of people in his company who, literally, want Jeff's time and expertise. Years ago he had given up on the notion that he could serve everyone.

Still, he is regarded as a model of productivity. He filters his client calls, internal calls, and email; carefully manages his time; and occasionally churns out ideas in an internal ezine that is now posted on the company's web mail. He focuses his attention on his supervisors and largest clients. His time management skills have led to productivity awards, more plaques on the walls. And he works long hours. Each day his eyes become heavier. The eye fatigue that he used to feel at 5:30, he now feels at 1:30. His back problems are now chronic.

He said, "Work is simply not as exciting as it once was. I'm still good at my job, just to be clear. I still get swept up by what needs to be done, the emergency of the moment. And I'm good at cleaning up the problems. But this morning I had a really strange thing happen.

"As I drove toward the office I heard sirens. Then I saw several fire engines and rescue vehicles. I smelled smoke. And while I was sitting at a red light, I pondered, 'What if our building had burned down? What if the company, and all the servers, all of it were gone – just like that?'

"And guess what I did? It was pretty strange, really. I just exhaled and said aloud, 'That would be great!' And I knew that it would be great. No work, no stress. What a thought! Isn't that strange? Years ago, I would have run the red light just to check it out and make sure that our building was not on fire."

What if your building were on fire?

Faced with an emergency, wouldn't you do whatever you needed for your safety and for other people's safety? You might run for the doors and windows. You might bring out the valuables. You might help those who needed an arm for support. You might call your loved ones. You would move fast!

In short, wouldn't you gather the needed resources and respond to the crisis?

WHAT IF YOUR LIFE WERE ON FIRE?

If you are smelling smoke somewhere in your life, I wrote this book to help you move from awareness to taking action steps that will create extraordinary success in your life and work. This book will help you light a fire under yourself. It will help you nurture ideas, like flames, into focused movement. Perhaps you have had to "light a fire" under someone else. As a manager and a parent and small business owner, I've had to do so countless times. This book will help you add some passion to your life.

Where do you want to add some passion and adventure into your life?

This book is a call to immediate action. You can nurture flames into warmth and gentle movement toward your goals. You may only have a sense of a need for change. Like a vague smell of smoke. Or you may be ready to leap off the cliff into each activity in this book.

My belief is that you are resourceful and capable, fully able to improve your personal or professional life. If you haven't already done so, it will be useful for you to adopt that same belief as you read and do these activities.

YOUR SUPPORT STRUCTURE

Let's start by looking at who is currently in your support structure. Write as many names as possible in the following chart.

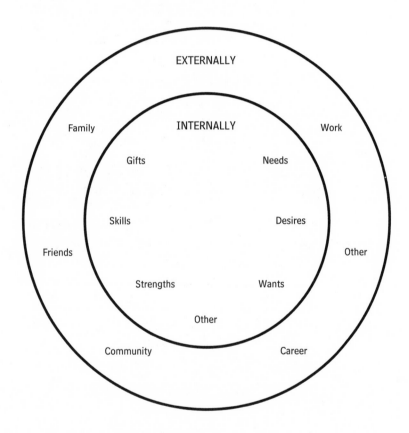

Your current support system is a snapshot limited by this moment in time. There may have been times when you had a larger support system. And there may have been times when it was smaller. The value in listing the names of those in your support system is that it provides you with a starting point.

A case in point is Teddy Roosevelt, who was known for passionate action. He loved wild adventures, especially in the American West. When talking about boxing, he said:

The credit belongs to the man in the arena, whose face is marred by dust and sweat and blood, who strives valiantly...who knows the great enthusiasms, the great devotions, who spends himself in a worthy cause....

Those words can also be applied to you, at this starting point.

YOUR PASSIONATE ACTION GOALS LIE AHEAD

You will define the terms of your adventure. It may include sweat and tears as you push and pull away from the familiar. It may include clients and endless meetings and a schedule that you cannot control. It may include children and shovels and roses and your backyard. It may include brooms and pans and used clothing and serving others at work or volunteering. Your life of passionate action may be a secret. It may be internal and reflective and a quiet gift to yourself. It may be fleeting. And it may be public and filled with extraordinary success, rewards, or life-defining purpose.

You may notice that throughout this book there are references to adventure. That is because the word adventure has only positive connotations to me. Adventures require choice. The roots of the word mean both to go and to arrive. In a similar way, you are on an adventure to create more passionate action in your life.

This book is designed for:
1. Anyone seeking passionate action
2. Anyone helping others achieve passionate action

AN ETHICAL CHOICE

Here is a story involving an ethical choice. It is used in some job applications, and will help you think about how you make your decisions.

Imagine that you are driving your car through a storm at 11:00 p.m. and you come upon three people who need your help. The first person is an elderly woman who is about to die, and she needs comforting. The second person is your best friend, who once saved your life, and he needs you to return the favor. The third person is the ideal partner of your dreams, and she needs to be rescued. You have room in your car for only one other person, and have to make a choice within seconds. Who do you rescue and why?

You may want to take the elderly woman because she needs comforting and your car would provide shelter from the storm. If you have ever supported someone in their final moments, you may know how essential this choice could be.

You may want to choose your best friend because, after all, he did save your life. You feel you owe him. And you like him. And you could relive the experience of that storm for years of continued friendship.

You may choose to take the ideal partner of your dreams. Regardless of your love life, you may be yearning for that ideal partner. And you could never imagine leaving her on the side of the road.

Wouldn't it be helpful to have a five-step process that you could immediately use to help you make such a decision?

Take a moment now to explore your options in this example. Whom do you rescue and why? (Pause for a moment)

There is no "correct" answer. If you chose to comfort the elderly woman, you may value supporting others. If you chose to rescue your best friend, you may value your word. If you chose to embrace your ideal partner, you may value romance. Also, there may be multiple options. For instance, you could choose to give your best friend the car key. Then you could encourage your ideal partner to join him in the car. As they drove away, you could choose to comfort the elderly woman in the storm, in her final moments. The five steps in this book will help you separate feelings and actions so that you can make decisions that are consistent with your values. I call this Passionate Action.

THE PASSIONATE ACTION MODEL

The Passionate Action Model is a framework for you to take these five steps. It is a structured approach to creating extraordinary success in your life or your work. These five steps work. I have taught them for years to hundreds of people just like you. They define a process, a methodology, a way for you to live with more passion. The five steps in the Passionate Action Model are:

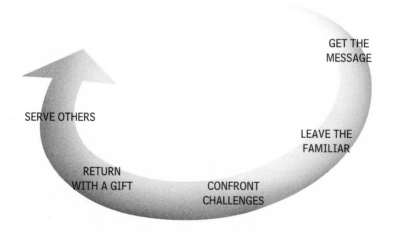

Each of these five steps is described in chapters 3-7. Each chapter is filled with practical activities, real-life examples from all walks of life, self-coaching techniques, provocative questions, models, ideas from other authors, and trail markers.

The Passionate Action Model is depicted in a circle because you will determine the starting point. It may not be step one for you. For instance, I recently presented this model in a seminar to business leaders. They started by writing about confronting challenges (chapter five). Then they wrote weekly goals into return with a gift (chapter six) and serve others (chapter seven). Then they paired up with someone and stated those points to each other. A basic skill in business – and in relationships – is to understand another person's main concerns. So, in that seminar, they helped each other get the message (chapter three) and determine how to leave the familiar (chapter two). Just as naturally, your starting point may be to get the message (chapter three) and you may then move forward as written.

There are many benefits of the Passionate Action Model. This model is:

- Easy to grasp. It is easy to understand these five steps. You should understand them quickly.

- Attractive. These steps may be attractive to you if you feel stuck or want to break away from current results.

- Familiar. These five steps are familiar in a mythic way to most people. Every hero myth or action movie includes these five steps.

- Useful. You may find that this model is a useful structure if you need a behavioral change, new start, or performance measurement such as return on investment.

- Effective. People do change. You can too. The Latin root for the word passion means to move past suffering.

■ Flexible. You can apply the Passionate Action Model to any aspect of your life and work. Many have applied it to personal goals, such as finding wealth or love. Others have applied it to professional goals, such as a career transition or selling a new project.

■ Multi-dimensional. The Passionate Action Model can be applied to many dimensions of your life, such as personal, athletic, or financial goals. It may also be applied individually to you, your family or work group, or to your organization.

The Passionate Action Model is based on the premise that each of us is on an adventure in life, and that we can influence some outcomes by making smart decisions. Sometimes your adventure, just like mine, leads to desirable choices. Sometimes those decision points do not seem at all desirable. Your adventure may have chaotic, muddy, cold, scary times, when you are not sure what to do next. Those are the times when you need to have a friend, or a coach, or your faith, or a support system. Those are the times when you need this guidebook.

When reading this book, you may want to focus on yourself at work. That may be where you spend much of your time, and your career may be fascinating. Alternately, you may want to focus on your home life, parenting, or interpersonal skills. Or you may focus on life goals such as balance, fulfillment, health, or finance. One of my friends is a stay-at-home father of five who has literally measured galaxies for NASA. He says, "Until our youngest is in school, this is my work. I cannot imagine doing anything else." His action goal includes being a great father.

Two case studies are described in chapters 3-7 so that you can notice changes that other people make in each step of the Passionate Action Model. These characters, Joel and Christy, are representative examples. You can use them like a mirror for reflections into your life, or like a window, as possibilities for your own Passionate Action goals.

TRAVEL TIPS

Before you take any leaps, get cold feet, or feel frozen, let me explain a few things. When mountaineers travel down the mountain, they pass along advice to novices about the challenges ahead. In the same way, when travelers abroad meet other travelers from their home, they share local wisdom and news. Here are some quick travel tips:

- Take your time. The forms, questions, and examples in the following pages are designed to help you take your time. Sample and savor them, as if at a long, sumptuous buffet. You control the pace of your reading.

- Add variety. Skip pages or scan the anecdotes and examples as you follow your energy. There are hundreds of ideas and activities ahead. Know that each one will help you learn something about yourself. There are many paths to your truth.

- Reward yourself along the way. When you complete a chapter or attain a Passionate Action goal, celebrate with a friend, a special event, or a gift for yourself!

- Keep going. There is always "just one more ridge to get over" and the goal is always "just around the next bend." Persistence counts.

- Push to the next level. Sometimes people train and train and wonder why they can't beat their personal record or make the next goal at work. Generally, they quit just before pushing through that last 5–10% of the project.

■ Notice the trail markers. Reflect periodically along the way in this book. You will find trail markers at the beginning of chapters 3-7.

WE DO NOT HAVE TO RISK THE ADVENTURE ALONE,
FOR THE HEROES OF ALL TIME HAVE GONE BEFORE US....
WHERE WE HAD THOUGHT TO TRAVEL OUTWARD, WE WILL
COME TO THE CENTER OF OUR OWN EXISTENCE.
AND WHERE WE HAD THOUGHT TO BE ALONE,
WE WILL BE WITH ALL THE WORLD.

– Joseph Campbell, *The Power of Myth*

CHAPTER 2

The Passionate Action Model

What if you knew that your adventure had some milestones, some steps that were similar to other great adventurers in the past? Their stories could inform yours. Their stories could be a useful model to you. Well, there is a useful model. This chapter starts with an ancient example. Then we will move to more contemporary examples.

■ PASSIONATE ACTION EXAMPLE #3

Thousands of years ago, there was a Greek island filled with walls and complex walkways. The people were terrified every nine years when they had to sacrifice 14 boys and girls to a monster, called a Minotaur, who lived in the center of this labyrinth. No one ever came out alive. Then one day a man from Athens came along. He got the message and thought, "There must be a pathway through these complex walls." So he volunteered to confront the Minotaur, a monster that was part human and part bull. He secured his father's blessing and a gift from the woman who loved him. She gave him a ball of string that he could unravel as he walked deeper and deeper into the labyrinth. And as he walked, he left the familiar world behind.

The young man confronted several challenges in the labyrinth. He nearly lost his path. He was tempted by his fears of the Minotaur. He fought and killed the Minotaur. The string guided him and the hostages out. He returned with a gift: the young people were alive and the town was freed from oppression. He then went back to Athens, and he spent his life seeking adventure and serving others. His name was Theseus, and he defined the course for Athenian democracy and individual liberty. Not a bad legacy.

I imagine that Theseus was excited and scared and fully alive. I imagine that he carried his goal in his heart and his sword in his hand. Just like you. Just like you and your Passionate Action goal.

You may be thinking: Well, that story was a long time ago. What does it have to do with me?

The short answer is, EVERYTHING! When each of us goes on an adventure, we experience these five steps of the Passionate Action Model. You must take each step, holding your goals in your heart and this book in your hand.

TRAVEL TIP

Chapters 3-7 address each of these five steps in detail. At the end of chapters 3-7, you will find a list of Action Items that work well. All of the activities are cross-referenced in the appendix. In this chapter we will use contemporary examples so that you can apply the Passionate Action Model to your life.

THE FIVE STEPS IN THE PASSIONATE ACTION MODEL

GET THE
MESSAGE

SERVE OTHERS

LEAVE THE
FAMILIAR

RETURN
WITH A GIFT

CONFRONT
CHALLENGES

THESE FIVE STEPS OF PASSIONATE ACTION
WILL HELP YOU TO:

1. Get moving when you feel stuck

2. Leave behind familiar habits or behaviors

3. Confront challenges with confidence

4. Return with a gift such as wisdom
   or compassion that can be applied
   to your life and work

5. Serve others in their lives

■ **PASSIONATE ACTION EXAMPLE #4**

Denise's career has been filled with achievement and restlessness. Her resume is filled with names of respected universities and companies where she has worked. Her achievements include an MBA, consulting career, directing community relations for a large symphony, and working as the executive director of a conservatory.

Privately, though, she is uncertain about her next career transition. She is accustomed to working 60+ hour weeks and having little time for personal interests. Denise has just accepted a new job that requires a move to New York City. She wants to create better balance between her work and personal life.

Denise is focusing on creating a new home. She has imagined what that home looks like. It must have space for her grand piano, leather reading chair, a window with a view, and high speed computer access. Her physical home is a symbol, an extension of herself, a place for rejuvenation and entertaining.

This career move is different for her, though. This time, she is motivated by a sense of mission rather than financial reward. She wants to work with a different clientele, people with lower financial means. She is now seeking fulfillment. Denise has a number of great friends in New York City. She even has a board of directors that will help her locate a home.

Her Passionate Action goal is specific: She wants to move into her new home and live a more balanced life. Her Passionate Action goal outline looks like the list on the right.

Just like you, Denise will have many goals happening concurrently. The value of applying any model is that you can focus on one Passionate Action goal at a time. Copy the following form onto different pieces of paper, one for each goal in your life. There will be overlaps. Use each piece of paper as a map for your Passionate Action goals.

DENISE'S GOALS

1. **Get the message**
   a. Work with different (lower income) clientele
   b. Seek a better balance of work and personal life

2. **Leave the familiar**
   a. Accept offer to move to New York City
   b. Determine characteristics of a home
   c. Determine characteristics of a rewarding personal life (hobbies, friends, etc.)

3. **Confront challenges**
   a. Work with friends and board members to find a good neighborhood
   b. Embrace challenges of the new job
   c. Create a fulfilling social life with new people

4. **Return with a gift**
   a. Select a home; move in
   b. Feel comfortable, centered, satisfied with self

5. **Serve others**
   a. Serve others at work
   b. Feel rejuvenated in personal life (entertaining and music)

Many people struggle to create work-life balance. Many people struggle to create a new home for the next phase of their life. Perhaps you are struggling, too. When you use the model to outline what you want, it can help you determine your starting point.

■ PASSIONATE ACTION EXAMPLE #5

Here is another example, from one of my coaching clients who works in a large company. His goal is to be more visible at work and be taken seriously at meetings. His Passionate Action goal outline looks the chart on the right.

CLIENT'S PROFESSIONAL GOALS

1. **Get the message**
   a. Be more visible at work
   b. Be taken seriously at meetings

2. **Leave the familiar**
   a. Change physical appearance, dress more colorfully
   b. Always ask for the meeting agenda before the meeting
   c. Prepare for each meeting by asking several colleagues specific questions about the subject

3. **Confront challenges**
   a. Practice speaking with confidence in private and in public
   b. Develop a physical trigger that leads to confidence when speaking
   c. Speak directly to others

4. **Return with a gift**
   a. Ask for tasks or responsibilities during meetings
   b. Set a speaking goal for each meeting (if cannot directly contribute to agenda items, then will indirectly contribute by complimenting a colleague's work)

5. **Serve others**
   a. State personal accountability status during meetings
   b. Confirm accountability status of colleagues during meetings
   c. Continue working toward goals of being more visible and being taken seriously at meetings

MY PASSIONATE ACTION GOAL OUTLINE

Directions: Select one goal in your life; complete each step as you progress through this book. Copy the outline for as many goals as you wish.

My Passionate Action goal is to:

_____

_____

_____

_____

_____

My Passionate Action goal looks like this:

1. Get the message

   a. _____

_____

   b. _____

_____

   c. _____

_____

2. Leave the familiar

   a. _____

_____

   b. _____

_____

   c. _____

_____

3. Confront challenges

a. _____

_____

b. _____

_____

c. _____

_____

4. Return with a gift

a. _____

_____

b. _____

_____

c. _____

_____

5. Serve others

a. _____

_____

b. _____

_____

c. _____

_____

TRAIL MARKERS AHEAD

TRAVEL TIP

This chapter will help you Get the Message by developing self-awareness and determining your action-based success goals. Just like packing for a trip, in this chapter you will gather the tools and resources you need. You may know exactly what your goal is. More often, just as one trail turns onto another ridgeline, you will adopt new goals. Getting the message requires your attention, some openness, listening, considering options, then selection of a Passionate Action goal.

CHAPTER 3

Get the Message

Frodo Baggins, the hobbit, did not want to leave the shire or carry a ring through dangerous lands. But he accepted endless challenges and finally returned the ring to the center of the earth.

Noah did not want to build an ark, and repeatedly questioned the need. Somehow, he got the message and his hard work led to the survival of all living beings.

Bill Gates, founder of Microsoft, believed that developing better software would lead to his vision of a computer on every desk. He combined strategy with opportunity and led countless others to take that message into a reality.

Jack Welch was called upon to develop General Electric into a global powerhouse. He faced many challenges from within the company and within the market, yet he prevailed and the company grew.

Like you, each of these people got the message.

PUSHING AND PULLING

Your Passionate Action goal exists for one of two reasons. You have either been pushed into it, or pulled into it.

PUSHING   YOU   PULLING

External forces push us into action. Often, we call them challenges. Perhaps a loved one has died in a car accident, leaving you alone, and you have been pushed to make crucial decisions that affect your survival. Perhaps you have lost your faith, or lost some financial support. Or, perhaps you have been forced to relocate your home. You may be as reluctant as Noah or Frodo. The push may be undesired, such as when a loved one becomes ill or when you are fired from a job. And the push may be desired, such as a promotion or windfall.

Internal forces also pull us into action. These internal forces may start as an undefined desire, urge, or feeling that pulls at you. Perhaps you know that something is lacking in your daily "normal" experiences of life, work, family, community. You may be questioning the value of your activities. You may be feeling bored or alienated in a sedentary, professional job that you had once thought could be special. Perhaps you are considering opportunities for early retirement, a career transition, a marital change. Over time, these internal forces become louder voices; they are pulling you into action.

Whether from pushing, pulling, or both, by defining these external and internal forces, you can get the message for possible actions.

One of my coaching clients used the following form to list what is pushing and pulling at him.

WHAT'S PUSHING AND PULLING?

PUSHING   PULLING

	PUSHING	PULLING
Career	I am not making enough money, financial demands.	I don't want to work within a corporation all my life.
Finances	I need to earn 10% more or cut my expenses by 15%.	I want to create a nest egg of $30,000.
Family	I should take better care of my retire parents.	I need to spent more time with my children.
Relationships		I want to develop better friendships.

That was his example. What about you? What are the external forces pushing on your life? What are your internal, intuitive voices saying?

SEEKING YOUR MESSAGE

You may not pay attention to the forces pushing and pulling at you. When you take a moment to list them, you may begin to realize that you have choices about what is influencing you. You may select a Passionate Action goal related to one of these forces.

Often I hear stories from people in transition who claim that they want to change some aspect of their lives. They may want a new job, new or better relationships, or a more fulfilling career.

Sometimes people want to share their thoughts out loud with a coach or an accountability partner, someone who supports their growth. You can create passionate action in any corner of your life, from talking to that person you dislike, to pursuing that hobby you love. And I have learned that each one of us is in transition, every day of our lives.

William Bridges, in *Managing Transition: Making the Most of Change*, distinguishes between these two words. He defines change as an external situation with a stop and a start, such as a new job, marriage, or home. A transition is your internal, gradual, psychological response to change. Transitions may include feelings from passion to excitement to fear.

As a species, humans are constantly evolving, responding to changes, making transitions, and gaining skills. You may find it useful to think of yourself as an athlete training for the next event. You may be a corporate athlete responding to the next business opportunity or threat. So, how do you develop self-awareness? First, you must ask some questions, then seek a message.

WHAT IS PUSHING AND PULLING
AT YOU IN YOUR LIFE?

Directions: Complete this form for each category. Add other categories as needed. Then circle the three most important forces pushing or pulling at you.

Career

_____

_____

_____

_____

_____

Finances

_____

_____

_____

_____

_____

Relationships

_____

_____

_____

_____

_____

Status

_____

_____

_____

_____

_____

Friends

_____
_____
_____
_____
_____

Comforts

_____
_____
_____
_____
_____

Leisure

_____
_____
_____
_____
_____

Physical Health

_____
_____
_____
_____
_____

Hobbies

_____

_____

_____

_____

_____

Other

_____

_____

_____

_____

What patterns emerge?

_____

_____

_____

Does one side have more notes than the other?

_____

_____

What kinds of messages are they?

_____

_____

_____

SOME QUESTIONS ABOUT THE MESSAGE

What bothers you?
What is lacking in your personal life?
What is lacking in your professional life?
What battles have you been fighting?
What battles are you avoiding?

WHAT WE SEEK, WE TEND TO FIND

"What we seek, we tend to find" may seem backwards from the biblical "Seek and ye shall find." But think of it as the next step of that idea. If you are seeking misery and depression, then you will find it. If you are seeking moments of joy, then you will find that, too. I know of a woman who had never seen a rainbow. She was amazed that I see them all the time. Once I explained that immediately after a rainstorm, you just need to go looking for rainbows, she did so.

For me, the passionate-action-based success process is filled with values including playfulness, uncertainty, risk, connection, and celebration. The most important is passion, because it extends from your values, provides energy, uses your strengths and leads to success. Ask yourself these two key questions. What are you passionate about? What makes you fully alive?

Sometimes when people feel stuck or are having trouble getting the message, they feel like victims of their situation. We each suffer losses from illness, careers, death, families, and friends. How you respond to those losses defines you. Do you believe that the life you are living is the life you have developed? Your current reality, however bright or dismal, is the sum total of all that you believe to be true. You have created that reality as a result of your beliefs and life choices.

Let me give you a personal example. I spent years living in dormitories, teaching high-school-aged students at boarding schools. Then I longed to work in a day school. Then I longed to be an administrator. Then I longed to start a business. This morning, when I noticed that my phone was not busy, I longed for more connection with clients. The main point is that the life I am living is the life I have developed. There is no mistake. Here is an example of another man in transition.

■ PASSIONATE ACTION EXAMPLE #6

Jacob had worked for the federal government for 36 years and loved many aspects of his job. He was reluctant to change. He commuted by subway for 80 minutes each day. He spent the time reading the complete works of one author before moving on to another. Over the years, his reading had become a sacred time, filled with curiosity and wonder.

Jacob was recently pulled into a life-changing experience. One evening, he was reading on the subway, as usual, fully en-grossed in his book. Suddenly the man sitting next to him slumped over onto his shoulder. Jacob looked over at the stranger. His mouth was open, his eyes were closed, and he was breathing deeply. The other man's body became heavier as he fell deeper into sleep. Jacob's mind swirled with a rush of possibilities. He could awaken the stranger; he could stand up and take another seat; he could push the stranger against the wall. Instead, Jacob stared at the dark window across the aisle. In the window was the reflected image of a dark lumpy mass of bodies and two faces. One face was awake and staring with a haunted look. The other face was asleep and slumped onto a shoulder, unaware of his im-pact on anyone or anything.

To Jacob, this image represented his fate, like a two-headed monster with no purpose. He got the message. Within months he retired, moved into the country, built a wood shop, and began making furniture. And he spent a month each summer canoeing in the Canadian wilderness.

When Jacob described this experience he said, "Frankly, I was terrified by the dark image in the window. It was a wake-up call for me. And I have had no regrets."

As a professional coach, I hear stories from people who are so overwhelmed that they do not see any choices. They are walking through a misty forest filled with rocks and streams. Their direction is unclear. They once had a map, or a compass, but those tools are broken. The branches in the nearby trees have intertwined, making them feel fenced in. They see no clear way to progress. Who do you know who is a little bit lost?

INVENTURES

Few of us can trek in the wilderness. However, each of us can embrace Passionate Action goals closer to home. Dick Leider describes "Inventures" as changes in your local environment that help you feel more alive. Assume for a moment that you are an experiment of one, and what you do depends on your environment and personal issues.

What would happen if you changed your internal environment on a regular basis? For instance, what would happen if every day for one week you:

- Spent ten minutes with a colleague you do not know very well

- Called an old acquaintance

- Ate ethnic foods from different restaurants

- Changed your morning wake up ritual

- Practiced complimenting five different people

What would happen if you did the following?

- Visited your chamber of commerce and asked members how and why they started their small businesses

- Visited an outplacement firm and asked those in the waiting room what they thought about jobs moving overseas

- Joined an Elderhostel group and encouraged the participants to share their stories, or did the same at an active retirement community center

- Visited a church and met six new people.

Would your heart race a bit, your eyes open, your adrenalin surge? Would you feel more alive – as if you were trekking in your local world? These inventures, these local actions, help you leap before you look. They lead to maximum aliveness.

These local actions may help you determine your Passionate Action goal. Or they may help you learn how you spend your time each day.

ONCE WE BELIEVE IN OURSELVES, WE CAN RISK CURIOSITY,
WONDER, SPONTANEOUS DELIGHT,
OR ANY EXPERIENCE THAT REVEALS THE HUMAN SPIRIT.

—e.e. cummings

▲ ACTIVITY: TIME LISTS

Directions: Complete the Actual Time List for an average day last week. Be honest. Then complete the Desired Time List for an ideal day next year. Notice the similarities and differences between the two lists you just completed. What is different between the two lists? In the Actual Time List, what times are invigorating or life enhancing for you? What times are draining or unnecessary for you? What times could lead to your Passionate Action goal?

TIME	ACTUAL ACTIVITY	TIME	DESIRED ACTIVITY
12 am	_____	12 am	_____
1 am	_____	1 am	_____
2 am	_____	2 am	_____
3 am	_____	3 am	_____
4 am	_____	4 am	_____
5 am	_____	5 am	_____
6 am	_____	6 am	_____
7 am	_____	7 am	_____
8 am	_____	8 am	_____
9 am	_____	9 am	_____
10 am	_____	10 am	_____
11 am	_____	11 am	_____
12 pm	_____	12 pm	_____
1 pm	_____	1 pm	_____
2 pm	_____	2 pm	_____
3 pm	_____	3 pm	_____
4 pm	_____	4 pm	_____
5 pm	_____	5 pm	_____
6 pm	_____	6 pm	_____
7 pm	_____	7 pm	_____
8 pm	_____	8 pm	_____
9 pm	_____	9 pm	_____
10 pm	_____	10 pm	_____
11 pm	_____	11 pm	_____

▲ ACTIVITY: MY PLACE OF POWER

Thoreau wrote "The mass of men lead lives of quiet desperation," about 150 years ago. His words still ring true. You may long for a refuge, a cabin at Walden Pond. When I was 23, I studied Henry David Thoreau while fasting for three days along a lake in Northern Minnesota, and I wrote some life goals for the first time.

How about you? Are you living a life of "quiet desperation?"

Imagine a place where you could retreat from all of the challenges of your life. It may be a physical place. Or your retreat may be an imaginary place. Mental health practitioners call this a "Safe Place." Once it is defined, their client may retreat to their safe place again and again. Similarly, Quaker educators ask children to describe a "Heart Room." This is the still, quiet, peaceful place within their heart that they can return to when threatened. Whatever the name, it is a place of power and resourcefulness for you.

Another useful exercise is to remember a peak experience, a time when you were tremendously effective or tremendously useful to someone. That memory is a place of power, a great resource for you. Recall all of the details related to that memory. Recall the words, sounds, your actions, how it felt. Use each sense to recall the details of that powerful memory: the sounds, sights, feelings, taste.

Now draw or write about those details. Capture it alone by yourself for at least five minutes. Use the space to the right or another piece of paper. Start your timer now!

When you are done, label this memory "My Place of Power" or "My Resource Place" or "My Heart Room." Use whatever title is helpful. Place that image, in words or drawing, in a prominent place. It will be a useful resource while you define your Passionate Action goal.

Some of my coaching clients take their sketch and place it near their office, so that they can be reminded of their place of power when they need it the most. Some place it in a briefcase, on a wall, in a private drawer, or on a laminated page. Others place their sketch in a digital format and recall it from their computer or cell phone or screen saver when needed.

MY PLACE OF POWER

▲ ACTIVITY: THINK IT AND INK IT

Here is another activity that will help you define your action-based success goal. When writers brainstorm, they follow the motto: "If you think it, ink it." Writers need to get it down on paper, out of their heads, before they can do any editing.

Think about your life and imagine living for at least 80 years. Create a timeline on a piece of paper and, as you think it, ink it – write notes about what you would like to do in each decade. What might you do at age 20, 40, 60, or 80? Use this timetable as a brainstorming activity.

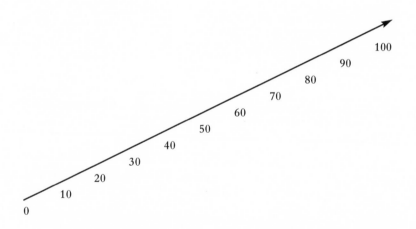

Perhaps you just revealed a Passionate Action goal. Is there something on that list that you have not yet done, but want to do before you die? Is there something that you once started and it remains unfinished?

Here is another way to think it and ink it. What would happen if you listed 101 of your life goals? These may be ambitious goals like "pay for my children's college education" or simpler life goals like "learn how to order a drink in Spanish." They could be interests that you want to do next year, or 40 years from now. The point is to think broadly and deeply. If you are lacking ideas after a day or two, start asking people about their hobbies or interests. You may want to write each goal on an index card.

Once you have a list of 101 possible life goals, then you can sort them. Start with a list of ten that are nearly impossible. Then list ten that are relatively easy to accomplish. Then list ten that would help others. Then list ten that would make money. Any one of these could become a Passionate Action goal for you.

If you brainstorm using either of these activities – the timeline or the list of 101 possible life goals – I know that you will trigger many possible ideas for your Passionate Action goals.

■ PASSIONATE ACTION EXAMPLE #7

Anyone can have a career change. On average, professionals currently change their careers five times. The next generation will change their careers at least ten times, and half of the careers that our children will pursue have not even been identified yet. Think of the possibilities for you!

I recently had a conversation with a physician who had always taken care of others. For years, in addition to her medical practice, she had written articles and set up virtual communities for people who could not afford direct medical care. She gave away her time and expertise. That was her pattern.

Last week, she resigned from her medical position because she felt called to write another book.

She said, "I wrote much of the first book ten years ago. Back then, I did not want to sell it because I wanted people to use it, without any excuses. Also, it may have been seen as a conflict of interest by my employer at the time. So I gave it away. I posted the content online and gave it away for free. Now I need to return to it. It is calling me back and must be my life's work."

Another physician friend of mine was on the U.S. Triathlon

team twice. He has just been asked to be president of his medical group. He has co-hosted bicycle races and adventure races. He recently moved into a new house, where he planted apple trees and installed a zip line for his daughters. I've know him for years as someone who always wants to do something else. He recently said that his next goal is to make the U.S. triathlon team one more time.

What might be your life's work?

Executive coaches at a top outplacement services company, Lee Hecht Harrison, support people who have been laid off from work. They are expensive. And their business is booming.

One general manager, a senior vice president, explained how important it is to get the message. He said, "Our clients need a sense of hope. They need to know that they have abilities and skill sets that are appreciated by others. They often feel bitterness or sadness or something negative about their previous employer. And they are aggressively seeking a better life."

Just like you.

There is more mystery and magic in the world than there are clear answers. Passionate Action based success requires that you walk in unfamiliar terrain, otherwise you are on a familiar stroll. If you are seeking a message from the spiritual world, it may be useful for you to do the following activities.

▲ ACTIVITY: DIVINE MESSAGES

In every culture through every age, people have needed time for reflection, meditation, prayer, faith.

Just imagine that you can hear an intentional calling from a divine source. This exercise may be a stretch for you, but my experience is that everyone can imagine such a divine voice. Start by sitting alone, in silence, and listen to your breathing. Imagine that

THE IMPORTANT THING IS NOT TO STOP QUESTIONING.
CURIOSITY HAS ITS OWN REASON FOR EXISTING.

– Albert Einstein

a divine source cares greatly about you, and has a message for you. If useful, start by focusing on the form of the divine source.

What does that divine source look like?
How does it communicate?
How does it make you feel?
How does it make others feel?
Now, what is the message?

One of my former clients is a great healer who uses angels in his practice. For years, he denied them. Now he accepts their messages and trusts that they will help him find the correct words.

Many years ago, I worked with the only Caucasian who was trained by the Lakota people in ancient rituals such as the vision quest and sweat lodges. After many years of study, this man knew the old ways of the shamans in the Black Hills of South Dakota. Then he shared those rituals in a sweat lodge ritual. It lasted about four hours. We began with chanting and drumming, and giving a token gift to the lodge. Then we recognized the seven cardinal directions, east, west, south, north, above, below, and the mystery within. The sweat had four stages, called doors. After each stage, we would either leave the lodge for a quick dip in a stream or cool down by walking outside. Then we would return for the next purification stage. Each stage consisted of prayers to those in our past, present, and future, and to friends in the animal and spirit worlds.

I was way out of my comfort zone while participating, and I hope that I never forget the images that came to me. I got the message that I needed to work in a community of people, not the wilderness. So within months, I made a career transition and moved to Chicago.

Do you recall times when you have felt a connection to a divine message or a spiritual energy?

I recall walking and praying in Salisbury Cathedral in England. The spires, statues of the saints, organ, and boys' choir practicing in the background transported me somewhere else. Then our guide brought us to a private portion of the nave. From there we could see the afternoon sunlight streaming through ancient stained glass images of Jesus and Mary and several disciples. We were encouraged to stay and pray. The group kept moving. I stayed for over an hour. Although I have visited hundreds of sacred places, my epiphany in that sanctuary remains strong. That is another place where I got the message that I was created to do great work with others.

▲ ACTIVITY: FUTURE SELF

Warning: this activity is powerful! Start by setting aside at least 15 minutes and resting in a quiet place, away from distractions. Close your door and turn off the phone. Have your coach or a friend read the following script to you.

Let yourself be surprised by this activity. There are many versions of this guided visualization; here is one script:

"Let your body physically relax, starting from your toes to your legs and torso, each arm, finally to your head. Imagine waves of white light or energy moving slowly up and through your body, then releasing tension past your head. They may be pulsing waves of light, like waves at the beach. Imagine any distracting thoughts flowing through your body, up and out, and leaving your head like raindrops, up and away.

"Now bring your attention to your eyes and imagine a third eye, between the other two. Imagine that this third eye has a beam of light emanating from it. Select a color for that beam. Imagine that it is extending out of this room, into the air, then into outer space. Follow that beam of light up and away, far from this country, this continent, this planet. Look back and notice that little ball of green and blue swirling around, Earth. Savor the view for a while.

"As you are looking around, notice another beam of light nearby. That second beam of light is also connected to the earth but it is a different color. Notice that color. Imagine yourself in this second beam of light and follow it through outer space, out of the darkness, closer and closer to Earth. Imagine returning to Earth 20 years from now. Notice the clouds, continents, countries, states, cities as you begin to land. Imagine yourself landing 20 years from now; notice what the year will be. Select a place to land. Notice where it is, some details around you. Imagine the building nearby.

"That building is where your future self lives... where you will live 20 years from now. Notice some details of the building. What does it look like outside? Notice the landscaping, doorway, driveway, the shape of the building. Get a feeling for this place. Do whatever you need to do to approach the door. Know that on the other side of the door will be your future self. Prepare yourself to be greeted by your future self, who is waiting just on the other side. Now open the door and say hello.

"As you open this door, notice what your future self looks like, how your future self moves, how your future self is dressed, how you feel around this person. Now imagine moving inside the house to a comfortable room and sitting down. Your future self invites you to feel comfortable, and you say whatever you need. Notice how it feels to be together.

"As you begin your conversation with your future self, you may want to start with your own questions. Let me give you a few questions first. Then you will have time to add your own questions. Start by asking, 'Future self, what do you remember most about the last 20 years? What stands out in your memory?' Take a moment now to hear the answer. (Pause here.)

"Now ask your future self another question; ask, 'What do I need to be most aware of in order to get from where I am to where you are? What would be most helpful for me to know?' Take a moment now to hear the answer. (Pause here.)

"Now take some time to ask your future self some of your own questions. What are some of your questions for your future self? Take some moments now to ask your questions and to hear the answers. (Pause here.)

"Now it is time for a final question and a request. Ask your future self, 'What name, other than your first name, are you called by? What is your sacred, private, powerful name? It may be a symbol or metaphor or strange sound. What is this name?' (Pause here.)

"If you had any trouble selecting a name, try this activity. Place both hands in front of you with your palms up and open. In your right hand, imagine all the animals in the world; select one animal that you feel connected to. Imagine that it speaks to you. In your left hand, imagine all the adjectives in the world. Then clap your hands, combine the adjective and the animal, and adopt that name.

"Good. Now is the time to share thanks and prepare to leave. Take some time to state your appreciation for the wisdom of this future self. If you want to, request a gift such as a small reminder of the visit. Make your way to the door and wave or say goodbye. Then find your way past the landscaping to that beam of light that brought you there. Before you leave, look back at the house and notice how it looks. Then follow that beam of light up and away, well above the building where your future self lives. Once again, move above the clouds and into outer space. When you notice that you are in the blackness again, glance back and see the little blue ball called Earth.

"Notice that once again there is another beam of light nearby. Step onto it. And again follow that beam of light down to Earth, back through the clouds to this present place. Return to this continent, this state, this town, and this building. Prepare to return back into this room in a few moments, when I count from 'three' to 'one'. When you hear the count of 'one,' you will be refreshed and ready to write some notes on the following page. Know that you will remember everything from this guided visualization.

"Now you are ready. Three, you are returning to the present time. Two, you are stretching your body, feeling the floor and gaining awareness of others around you. One, your eyes are open, you are refreshed and alert.

"Spend a few minutes now, writing some notes about your guided visualization activity."

NOTES ABOUT YOUR FUTURE SELF

Describe the building where your future self lives.

_____

_____

_____

_____

_____

_____

Describe how your future self looks and moves and makes you feel.

_____

_____

_____

_____

_____

What memory stands out for your future self from the last 20 years?

_____

_____

_____

_____

_____

What helpful advice does your future self offer you?

_____

_____

_____

_____

_____

What is the secret, powerful name of your future self?

_____

What gift did your future self offer you, or give you?

_____

_____

_____

What other questions did you ask your future self? What were some of the answers?

_____

_____

_____

_____

For many people, the future self gives advice to the present self. The future self can give you the message. For instance, the future self can tell you what to let go of when striving for passionate action. Or, the future self can encourage you to see your gifts and strengths. Let your future self be an active guide. You created that image. You can return at any time and ask again, until you get the next message.

ASSESSMENT INVENTORIES

Are you still wondering how to get the message? Many of us live in a world where data speaks louder than divine messages. We are forced to make cost benefit analyses. If the numbers warrant an investment in venture X, then we spend the time and money making X happen. That process defines good business sense.

Everyone can benefit from objective data. In the world of human development, we depend upon such data from our physicians and medical professionals. These experts can tell us when we need to reduce the risk of heart disease, lose weight, exercise more, control diabetes, or take medication. When the benefit outweighs the cost, then we go visit the doctor or have that operation.

In the business world, we also get data from our customers and colleagues every day. They either buy our products and services, or they don't. When they enjoy working with us, there will be rewards such as continued business, a bonus or promotion.

However, for most people, there is a lack of objective data. Assessment inventories are the best way to learn about your strengths and weaknesses. Think of them as questionnaires that help you become aware of what you know to be true about yourself. Several are described below.

If you are seeking a self-assessment, turn to the appendix or go to www.action-learning.com. You will learn where your strengths lie in four domains. Think of these as four directions. These domains are familiar to you:

1. Physical domain
2. Emotional domain
3. Cognitive domain
4. Spiritual domain

Within each of these domains there are four ways to develop action-based success: self-awareness, self-care, social awareness, and social contribution. Think of these as areas for attention. You may not need to develop self-care in your physical domain, for instance, if you are already taking great care of your body and living environments. For most people, though, there are areas for attention or development. This assessment inventory only takes a few minutes, and will help you determine your areas for attention. In chapter six there are dozens of examples of practices, ways to develop more passionate action in your life.

YOUR HOMEWORK

Turn to the appendix and take this assessment right now. It will help you define your action-based success goals.

Here are four other assessment inventories that will help you learn about your strengths and weaknesses. The MBTI (Myers-Briggs Type Inventory) defines 16 basic types of preferences based on the research of Carl Jung. The dominant categories are extroversion-introversion, sensory-intuition, feeling-thinking, and judging-perceiving. It is available from CPP online.

The DISC assessment describes how one responds to problems (Dominance), people (Influence), pace (Steadiness) and procedures (Compliance). It leads to two graphs: your natural and your adapted behaviors. It is available from Target Training International or Carlson Learning.

The Insight Inventory also leads to two graphs; these are graphs of your work style and personal style. The dominant categories are direct-indirect, outgoing-reserved, steady-urgent, and precise-unstructured. It is available from HRD Press.

The Clifton Strengths Finder is the result of Gallup researchers' study of successful people, and the book *Now, Discover your Strengths* focuses on sales managers and sales professionals. However, its value extends well beyond business. The assessment defines your top five talents among 34 themes, and it is available at the Gallup organization

The results from any of these assessment inventories should help you get the message. They should help you define your Passionate Action goal. Complete at least one of these inventories immediately.

CASE STUDIES

Hopefully, Christy and Joel have traits and opportunities that are similar to yours. Use these case studies after the next five chapters to focus on your action-based success. After each case study, there are some sample questions to help you get your message.

✱ CASE STUDY A: CHRISTY

Christy is a stay-at-home mother of three school-aged children. Her husband works in a career that interests him and provides enough revenue for them to do some home improvements and to travel on vacation for about two weeks each summer. She is now 39 and just not sure what is exciting about her life. Unlike many of her neighbors, she is not interested in watching Oprah or volunteering for the PTA. She is supportive of her children in school and athletics, but during the day when they are gone, her desire is to do something more.

For years, Christy has used that time to work out at the nearby sports club. She has taken almost all the classes offered, from spinning to water aerobics. Christy is trim and can bench press 100 pounds.

The daytime hours are not as long as she would like. After cleaning the house and doing chores, she usually works out for 1–2 hours, does whatever shopping is needed, then greets the children when they come home from school. For the past 12 years, she has usually cooked dinner and greeted her husband when he returns home from work. Sometimes she thinks that she is just like her mother.

Christy recalls the busy days of college and the graphic design work she did full time for six years before getting married and having children. She liked being busy. She liked taking care of customers. Since having kids, she has expressed her creativity by painting some of the walls with murals of Winnie the Pooh, then soccer players. They were fun projects, but just a hobby.

Christy said, "My house is tidy, the clothes are neatly stacked in each of the kid's rooms. We have a healthy family, and I know that I should be happier. But I'm restless. Bored. Just not sure what is next in my life. My girlfriends are too much like me – all married with kids and similar hobbies. Sometimes I wish I could just run away from it all." She is seeking some kind of direction; she needs to get the message.

Some questions for you include:
What do you like about your present lifestyle?

How would you like things to be different?

What resources do you need (time or people or money) to create the change you desire?

What are small steps that you could take this week to add some passionate action to your life?

After doing the Future Self or other activities described in this chapter, how do you describe yourself in 20 years?

✱ CASE STUDY B: JOEL

Joel is a salesman. Every time you ask, "So, how is it going?" he shouts back "Excellent!" He dresses well, is always on time for meetings, and is handsome. When he tells stories, people usually lean forward. He likes to laugh. He loves to see others laughing. Joel lives with two other guys. They watch sports on the weekends.

In college, Joel played soccer and he liked being one of the boys. He ran hard. He enjoyed working on a team to reach a goal. He enjoyed the physical contact, getting hit while going for the ball. In the last ten years, he has volunteered as a soccer coach. He still kicks the ball around, but he no longer leads the sprints. His teams do well. He works out at a nearby health club about twice each week.

Joel is making money, saving money, but not making as much money as he wants. He practices saying different scripts, different lines with different kinds of clients. Sometimes they work. Sometimes they ring false. He hates phone rejection. It makes him feel insecure and alone. He doubts his ability to make the numbers.

Joel has dated many women, but never found the right one. Although he believes that she is out there, he is not holding his breath. In fact, he is losing faith that he will find her. He is lonely. He thinks sales is a good career, but he is not certain.

Some questions for you include:
What do you like about your present lifestyle?

How would you like things to be different?

What resources do you need (time or people or money) to create the change you desire?

What are small steps that you could take this week to add some passionate action to your life?

After doing the future self or other activities described in this chapter, how do you describe yourself in 20 years?

Now is the time to review this chapter.

YOUR ACTION ITEMS ARE

1. Complete the forms and activities above.

2. Reflect on this chapter before reading ahead.

3. Take some notes in the margin of this chapter as you review it; write some notes on each page. Write questions. Write down several messages.

4. Create adventure by fasting for one day. Start by listing at least ten habits that you are accustomed to doing in the course of the day. They may range from foods to drinks, activities, work habits, recreation. Select one habit that is a familiar part of your day, something that you could eliminate for one day without losing your job. Then fast from that habit for the day. Notice the feelings of discomfort and excitement.

5. Complete the Passionate Action Assessment Inventory in the appendix. Right now!

6. Fill in the following and transfer to page 22.

My Passionate Action goal is...

TRAIL MARKERS AHEAD

TRAVEL TIP

This chapter is about moving from awareness to action, packing your bags and leaving town. Leaving the Familiar is the most difficult step in the Passionate Action model. It will be helpful for you to take notes along the way and for you to do the activities ahead. Then reflect as you read. That way, you can travel with more intention, confidence and passion!

CHAPTER 4

Leave the Familiar

Small steps lead to larger steps. Do you ever wonder how you could include small steps into your day? In *A New Adventure Every Day*, David Silberkeit provides hundreds of examples, in several directions, including career, finance, on the home front, within your body, and in relationships. Specific examples range from volunteering at a nonprofit to leaving your watch at home.

The point is to commit to unfamiliar action. This chapter is the place for packing your suitcase or your backpack. Not with gear or clothing. But with the tools you need to help you create extraordinary success.

One of my favorite quotes is from the movie The High Adventures of Buckaroo Banzai: "Just remember, wherever you go, there you are." The protagonist, Buckaroo Banzai, thought that he needed to crash airplanes in order to enter the next dimension of space and time. After many crashes, he learned otherwise. Like Buckaroo Banzai, some people travel through a lifetime without leaving familiar ground. A similar maxim is, "If you keep getting what you don't like, then you need to start doing what you haven't done."

Since we cannot get away from who we are, if you don't like who you are, then you need to change who you are.

In many ways, you are forced to leave the familiar. In utero, you may have thought the world was warm and wet. Then you were shocked into another world. In childhood or adolescence, you may have thought that loved ones would always care for you. Then you learned that the world can be hard. Each of these examples is a step into the unfamiliar. You experienced puberty and became an adult. You left your family of origin and found your purpose. Parents nurtured you, then gave you wings. Adults supported you as much as they could, then they left familiar patterns. Families. Careers. Marriages. Illnesses. Retirements. And then you will be faced with death, the least familiar territory of all. Throughout your life, you are continually facing unfamiliar ground.

Regardless of your Passionate Action goal, it will be necessary for you to leave the familiar comfort zone. Start by considering what is familiar to you, then you can consider what you could live without.

SOME QUESTIONS ABOUT THE FAMILIAR

Describe your morning ritual. What happens when one aspect of that morning ritual is absent, like when you do not shower?

What do you do now, that you did exactly the same ten years ago?

What is some physical activity that you cannot imagine doing?

How do you like to be addressed by your loved ones?

What is something that you cannot imagine ever saying to your boss or supervisor? What situation would make you say it?

For many people, the games they played as a ten-year-old child are related to activities they love, or values they hold dear as adults. What games did you love to play when you were ten years old?

What could you absolutely, positively, not live without?

A JOURNEY IS LIKE A PERSON IN ITSELF: NO TWO ARE ALIKE.
AND ALL PLANS, SAFEGUARDS, POLICING, AND COERCION ARE FRUITLESS.
WE FIND AFTER YEARS OF STRUGGLE THAT WE DO NOT TAKE A TRIP;
A TRIP TAKES US.

–John Steinbeck, *Travels With Charley*

▲ ACTIVITY: TAKE A VISIT

This activity is based on an old story, one that you can apply to any possible action, in any location. I have used a beach location because it is full of natural beauty, power, movement, and possibility. Here's the story:

Once upon a time there was a woman who could not find much purpose to her life. She was filled with uncertainty. Her family, friends, work, even familiar activities, just felt meaningless to her. Her husband thought she was depressed. So she went to her physician, who listened to her describe her symptoms. The wise physician asked, "When you were a child, what was something that you loved to do?"

She paused, then said, "I enjoyed visiting the ocean."

"Okay, then," said the physician, "I think I can help you. However, you must agree to do what I write down for one day. Will you do so?" She agreed. Then he reached for his prescription stationary and wrote the following. "Tomorrow I want you to spend a full day, from 9:00 a.m. to 6:00 p.m. visiting the ocean. You may bring a simple lunch and water, but no books or other distractions. I will give you four prescriptions that will cure you if you follow them to the letter. Do not open the envelopes until tomorrow at the times noted on the envelopes. Those times are 9:00 a.m., 12:00 p.m., 3:00 p.m. and 6:00 p.m." With written instruction and envelopes in hand, she left his office.

The next day she drove to a nearby ocean and by 9:00 arrived at an empty beach. The wind was gusting, waves were crashing; she felt cold and forlorn. At 9:00 she opened the first envelope. It stated only one word, "Listen." And so she did, for three hours. She listened to the gulls and crashing waves, and the wind. In time, she centered into the place and listened to her thoughts as they wandered like those gulls.

At 12:00 she opened the next envelope and it, too, had a simple message. It said, "Reach back," and so she nibbled on her lunch and let her thoughts wander back to her youth and pivotal points in her life. At times she smiled, at other times she cried. The hours passed quickly as she recalled low points and high points that had brought her to that moment.

At 3:00 she opened the third envelope. It said, "Re-examine your motives." The afternoon hours were filled with deep emotions as she explored her reasons for living, her purpose, and what a life of fulfillment could look like. Her eyes wandered from the sand and waves up to the clouds as she watched the sun departing.

Finally, at 6:00 p.m. she was ready to leave. The day had been endless at times, much more emotional than she had expected. She opened the last envelope and read the final prescription, "Write your worries in the sand." Without hesitation she stood up and grabbed a stick. She walked toward the smoothest sand and wrote line after line. Just like her thoughts and feelings during the day, her writing was fast and easy at times, then slow and hard at other times.

She finally threw away the stick and looked back upon the sand. It was covered with scratched letters, like so many footprints by sandpipers or water birds. She smiled, then walked away, back toward her car. And as she did, she heard the largest wave crash upon the beach.She looked back. Then she laughed. The incoming tide had erased her words.

INSTRUCTIONS FOR THE TAKE A VISIT ACTIVITY

Write the following four messages, seal them in four envelopes, label the time, and give them to yourself or your client. This activity can be done in any location, by anyone, at any time. Individuals or couples in a relationship can also leave the familiar using this activity.

9:00   Listen
12:00   Reach back
3:00   Re-examine your motives
6:00   Write your worries in the sand

I SHALL BE TELLING THIS WITH A SIGH

SOMEWHERE AGES AND AGES HENCE:

TWO ROADS DIVERGED IN A WOOD, AND I –

I TOOK THE ONE LESS TRAVELED BY,

AND THAT HAS MADE ALL THE DIFFERENCE.

–Robert Frost

▲ ACTIVITY: QUICK EXERCISES

Remember Buckaroo Banzai? In order to leave the familiar, it helps to know where you want to go. In *The Fifth Discipline Handbook*, Peter Senge explains that we need to explore the tension between the current realities and our vision. The key question is: Where are you now, and where do you want to go?

Try this quick exercise. Place both of your hands in front of you, one palm up, one palm down, with about eight inches of space between them. The lower hand represents your current reality. The upper hand represents your vision. Imagine that a giant rubber band is looped around both of your hands. There is slight tension between your hands. When the current realities, the stressors, bog us down, we lower our hand, which lowers our vision. We have to do so in order to deal with those heavy realities! Conversely, when we extend our vision over the fence, into the stars, that same tension pulls our current realities to a higher level. That tension is a balancing act between our hands, between our current realities and our visions.

Here is a similar example using your body. Try standing on one leg. Then raise one arm over your head. As you do so, you will correct your balance again and again. That is an example of another type of balance in your life. You will correct yourself again and again in order to maintain a familiar, physical balance.

▲ ACTIVITY: THE BALANCE WHEEL

Many people seek balance in different aspects of their lives. The following model is one of the most common ways to understand where you are and where you want to go. And it is effective. The self-awareness that results from the balance wheel can help anyone develop mastery at the next level.

Directions: Each of these sections in the wheel of life can be used to quickly assess the balance in your life. Imagine that the center of the wheel represents the number 0 (least) and the perimeter represents the number 10 (most). For each category, draw a line that represents your level of satisfaction with your current reality. For instance, if you are not satisfied with your career, and would rate that a 2/10, then place a line 2/10ths of the way out from the center of the wheel. Continue assessing and marking lines for each category.

How balanced is your wheel?

_____

_____

_____

What categories are you fairly satisfied with?

_____

_____

_____

What categories are you dissatisfied with?

_____

_____

_____

MY CURRENT BALANCE WHEEL

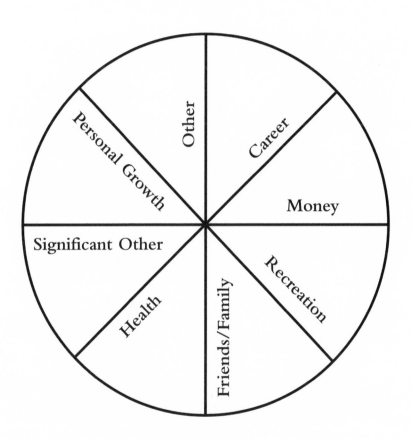

MY IDEAL BALANCE WHEEL

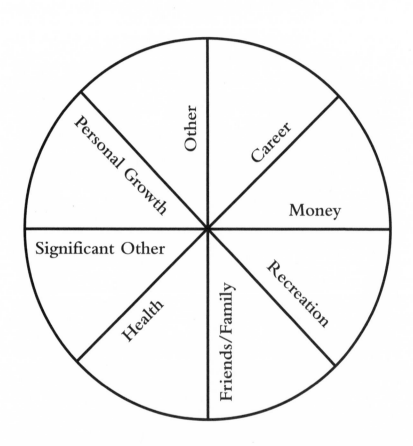

THE BALANCE WHEEL FOR YOUR IDEAL LIFE:

Directions: Notice that this second wheel has the same categories. This time, focus on your ideal life, how you would like things to be in your life. Then draw a line for each category that represents your level of satisfaction with that ideal. For instance, if your ideal level of satisfaction with career would be a 6/10, then place a line 6/10ths of the way out from the center of the wheel. Continue assessing and marking each category.

How balanced is your ideal wheel?

_____

_____

What scores are different from the current reality wheel?

_____

_____

What scores are the same as the first wheel?

_____

_____

How much do you want to move from the first wheel (current realities) to the second wheel (ideal life)?

_____

_____

What categories would you like to add or delete?

_____

_____

This activity can be used with countless labels. Select your own labels. Stephen Covey, in *The Seven Habits* series of books, calls these categories "Principles," and they may include: money, work, possessions, pleasure, friends, enemies, church, self, spouse/significant other, family. He explains that when you live a principle-centered life, you will spend more time and energy on the actions that you know are important.

You may be thinking that there must be balance in each of these categories. That is not necessary. If, for instance, you are not satisfied with your family because you are tending to a loved one with a terminal illness, then you know there is a lack of balance. You also know that imbalance will change when your loved one dies. What matters most is that we use the wheel of life as a snapshot, as a model that helps us recognize what is familiar and what needs to change.

The balance wheel of life can also be used as a diagnostic group activity. To do so, mark categories on the floor; use masking tape or file folders so that it looks like a wheel. Have people move from one category to the next and leave a post-it with their name in each category. For instance, if the category is "career," and you have someone in a 2 and someone else in a 10, the person who rated herself a 10 may be a good support person or coach for the person who rated herself a 2.

Passionate action into unfamiliar terrain requires that you take risks. You may need to step off the cliff, onto the boat, or under the water. Sometimes you will feel comfortable with the risks, sometimes you will need to understand them better.

▲ ACTIVITY: RISK TAKING AND RISK AVOIDANCE

So how do you know what steps to take? What trails are too dangerous, too risky? What risks will lead to injury? What risks will lead to jubilation?

I am not advocating dangerous activities, necessarily, but passionate action occurs on the edge of the mountain. That is where the view is.

Are you climbing on the edge of the mountain, or are you sipping a drink at the base camp lodge?

When you flip a coin, there are two sides, either heads or tails. So it is with risks. Risk may be defined as your deliberate choice to magnify positive consequences (risk taking) or to minimize negative consequences (risk avoidance) with a lower probability of gain. There is a chance of both positive and negative outcomes. Ultimately, you invest in that mutual fund, or buy that lottery ticket, or write that detailed email, because you believe there will be positive consequences ahead. You take the risk because you believe the positive consequences outweigh the negative consequences.

Risk avoidance is the opposite side of the coin. You decide not to act because the negative consequences outweigh the positive. Whether you take the risk or avoid the risk, each is a decision to act.

We take risks and avoid risks every moment of every day. You may choose the risk of taking the short cut at night through Central Park in New York City. You may avoid the risk of riding with a particular taxi driver because of his appearance. Our choices may be well considered or impulsive, unpopular or common responses to others, illegal or socially constructive, useful or destructive. The best way to assess risk is by using a continuum, or scale. Take a minute to complete these risk scales on the following page:

Of course there is danger; but a certain amount
of danger is essential to the quality of life.
I believe the risks I take are justified
by the sheer love of the life I lead.

–Charles Lindbergh

Rate your willingness to take risks at work:

(low)   1   2   3   4   5   6   7   8   9   10   (high)

Rate your willingness to take risks in relationships:

(low)   1   2   3   4   5   6   7   8   9   10   (high)

Rate your willingness to take illegal risks:

(low)   1   2   3   4   5   6   7   8   9   10   (high)

Rate your willingness to take impulsive risks:

(low)   1   2   3   4   5   6   7   8   9   10   (high)

There is a common quotation, "A ship in harbor is safe, but that is not what a ship is designed for."

If you are honest, you might admit that you have reduced the element of risk in your life. You may seek physical comforts in front of your computer or television screen or in your kitchen. You may add emotional comforts in your words or visits, and you may rarely experience an adrenalin-surging response to danger. If you did so, such as when a threat emerges, you may be quick to respond. In less than a second, your heart rate can increase 55 beats per minute, and you can have hormonal changes that enable you to fight, or to freeze, or to run away from the risk.

How would you rate your degree of risk taking?

_____

_____

_____

What risks are exciting to you?

_____

_____

_____

What risks are scary to you?

_____

_____

_____

What risks are connected to your spiritual calling?

_____

_____

_____

FACING GREMLINS

Throughout history, we have used maps to define the edges of the known world from the unknown, unfamiliar world. At that edge, our ancestors drew wild-looking dragons. They scribbled the warning, "Beyond this point there be dragons." Can you imagine what would happen if you were to draw or sketch that dragon in full color so that someone else could understand it?

When you give something unknown or unfamiliar a name and a body, then it becomes easier to confront. In *Taming the Gremlins*, Rick Carson calls this process "confronting the gremlin voices." Gremlins are haunting voices that reinforce negativity or doubt. We each have gremlin voices. Gremlin voices may say, "No, you can't do that!" or "Just who do you think you are?" These are the voices that prevent you from leaving the familiar.

PLAY FOR MORE THAN YOU CAN AFFORD TO LOSE,
AND YOU WILL LEARN THE GAME.

–Winston Churchill

Can you imagine a gremlin that scares you? It may say, "You can never be that successful!" or "You can never lose that much weight!"

You can look at that gremlin voice, or the gremlin monster, in two ways. One way is fearsome, and the gremlin looks invincible. But the other way to see the gremlin is through its vulnerability. And for that, you need to use some courage.

I love the quote "On the other side of fear is courage." Did you know that the word courage means from the heart? When you act with a little courage and step toward a fear, you are living with a full heart. When you face the vulnerable sides of the gremlin, you are fully into your passionate action, fully alive. Just like when Theseus carried his sword in his hand and left his fears behind.

Humor may help you gain courage. Do you have the courage to giggle at the wart on the nose of that gremlin?

One of my clients said it more specifically: "In my business, absolutely nothing is familiar. We have expanded, downsized, and been told that we are 'right-sized,' whatever that means. We've changed strategic goals so often; I can't recall how many times we have changed prospective clients. We have even changed buildings. Whatever the old ways have been, even five years ago, they just don't work any more. None of us knows if our new goals will work, but we do not have any choice. We must shoot from the hip. We have to trust our intuitions and make decisions. We must innovate. Our business is a series of actions, as we test one process after another."

■ PASSIONATE ACTION EXAMPLE #8

Do you ever long to break away from everything familiar and push against the odds?

The 2003 Adventure Racing National Championships were in the Sierra Nevada Mountains, between Yosemite National Park and Sequoia National Park. In July, my teammates and I had qualified for this endurance race by placing in a 48-hour race near our home in Washington, D.C. However, none of my teammates were able to travel to California for the national championships in November. There was no prize money involved in this amateur race. I was not convinced that I could find another group of fun, fast people as teammates.

In September, I called everyone I knew, asking for leads on prospective teammates. There are so many things that could go wrong! Teammates need to have a similar pace. They need to trust each other. They need to balance special skills, from navigation to bicycle repair. They need to have the gear and an optimistic mindset. They must be physically healthy in a sport that invites injury. They must be able to pay their own way. Ideally, they should have local information about the course area. Plus, we were required to have a support person who could transport four bicycles and a mountain of gear from one transition area to the next. That person would need to stay awake all night and prepare hot water in case we were hypothermic.

The weather was another major concern. The race was supposed to start at a ski area at 10,000-feet elevation. It usually snowed by mid-November. How could we bicycle, run, and paddle in deep snow?

These external challenges were small problems compared to the doubts raging in my head. I could stay at home and work. I could stick with the familiar. I thought about the saying, "If you spend all your time doing the same thing, that's what you'll get, the same old thing." I got the message; I decided to leave the familiar.

Within weeks, I had found a dream team of experienced racers, all from California. However, none of us had ever raced together. Jon had never been in an adventure race before. Melissa was only 24 years old. Ken had not completed a race that season and wondered if he was jinxed. We talked a bit on the phone, individually. I created a virtual team building form and we shared funny stories on email. Then my doubts increased – would we get along well enough? Could I race competitively with such a team?

Despite the unfamiliar challenges, we each made the commitment, had endless conversations about logistics and gear, made complicated travel plans, and exchanged cell numbers. Then we met at the Fresno airport, attended the race briefing, and began sorting gear. We sat down for spaghetti and a discussion of roles and expectations. Nothing was familiar. We were creating the expectations that would govern our travel.

As we feared, there was 6" of snow on the ground. The race director did not properly locate two of the checkpoints. Our success resulted from the fact that we shared the major decisions, like navigation. And we supported each other when two people were hypothermic.

We raced hard and finished 7th. Our team, Team Action-Learning.com, was ranked one of the best in the country! Like any other work team, we were committed to a goal. We met as strangers. We learned to travel in unfamiliar terrain, through the snow, dark, water, and mountains.

Just like you, we started with what we thought might lead to success in an unfamiliar adventure, made some small steps, then raced for a goal. We got to know each other. We learned that we could succeed. And we have subsequently applied those lessons to every other aspect of our lives. For a witty race description, written by Ken, visit the articles at www.action-learning.com.

BASELINE TABLES

Athletic coaches have expertise that can be applied to anyone who is leaving something familiar. The main idea is to start with a baseline, determine the current situation, and then use that data to chart desired changes.

Chris Carmichael was the coach for bicycle-racing legend Lance Armstrong. Lance won seven consecutive Tour De France

LIFE IS EITHER A DARING ADVENTURE OR IT IS NOTHING.

–Helen Keller

championships. However, Carmichael initially said that Lance was uncoachable, unwilling to listen, unwilling to work with a cycling team, unaware of just how good he could be. The story of Lance's relationship with his coach is documented in several books, including *The Ultimate Ride* and *The Lance Armstrong Performance Program*. Lance's out-spoken youth, rugged sprinting style, and his eventual World Championship demonstrated his passionate commitment. Despite his near fatal battle against cancer, he came back against all odds, eventually winning in races, in marriage, and in parenting. His crisis and his comeback are the stuff of passionate action.

Carmichael used coaching techniques to define a baseline of performance in the cycling world. Those measures included sprint times uphill, sprint times over distance, aerobic capacity, anaerobic threshold, muscle density, percentage of body fat, weighing all food for years, plotting all training and activity. However, because of all these demands, Lance was losing interest and even had to be talked into training. Somehow, during a rainy, cold training ride in the Appalachian Mountains, something changed for Lance. He describes his epiphany as the moment when he realized his training would help him reach the next level. He set his sights on winning his first Tour de France.

Like an athlete, all organizations have criteria for success. Companies may measure new sales, production costs, delivery time, employee retention, employee and client satisfaction. Nonprofit organizations may measure new members, service delivery hours, number of members served, commitment to an operating principle or value. The point is to select the data categories that you need in order to define a baseline. Then you can document the changes.

For example, a Fortune 500 company recently developed an executive coaching program and hired a third party to assess the value of the program. They found a 529% return on investment and significant intangible benefits to the business. When they included the financial benefits from employee retention, the overall Rate of Investment (ROI) jumped to 788% (Anderson).

What are the categories for your baseline table?

For athletes, you may want categories including base training, intensity training, peak training, racing, and recovery. In *SERIOUS Training for Endurance Athletes*, Rob Sleamaker and Ray Browning explain that components of each workout need to include speed, endurance, race pace, intervals, over-distance, uphill intervals, and strength conditioning. These components can be an example, or a metaphor, for you if you are not a superb athlete.

Your baseline table may include other assessment categories such as finances (revenue, assets, expenses), career (time spent working, income, degree of satisfaction, prospects), relationships (friends, family, spouse/significant other), recreation (hobbies, entertainment, time spent, money spent, degree of satisfaction), survival needs (eating, sleeping, loving, exercising). If you are seeking examples, refer back to the labels you used for the balance wheel of life.

Perhaps a detailed example will be helpful. One of my clients was a salesman with conflicting interests that were causing anxiety and erratic work performance. He wanted to have better balance between work and home. His wife wanted him to make more money. He also wanted to spend more time at the sports club, improving his tennis game. In college, he had been a great tennis player. He was concerned about maintaining his health. So when we started our coaching, he created a baseline table that looked like the one on the next page:

My Categories	Time Invested	Money Invested	Other Resources Invested	ROI	Notes
Work/Making Money	45 hrs per week		Car, Travel, Phone, Health	Salary, Ability to care for family	Draining but some advantages
Family Time	3hrs per day, 20+ hrs on weekends	Almost everything	Emotional Energy	Feel connected to loved ones	
Health Recreation	3-4 hrs per week	$100/ mo	Time away from family	Helping body	Frustrated that I can't play more

Remember Buckaroo Banzai? What you decide to do, your categories, will define where you are, your baseline table. For this client, the simple act of writing what he was doing most of the time helped him objectify his conflicting interests. Later he used that baseline as a reference.

What will you decide to do next? Your answer will define your successes ahead.

⁎

▲ ACTIVITY: MY BASELINE TABLE

Activity: Complete the following form using your categories so that you define a baseline. These are the familiar aspects of your life, prior to your next Passionate Action goal.

My Categories	Time Invested	Money Invested	Other Resources Invested	ROI	Notes

Before reading ahead, look back at that baseline table for a second. This is an important list! This table represents your current habits, how you spend your time and money. Those habits are based on what you value. You may value time with your children, and notice that there is not a large revenue number on the right side of the table. You may value building your business and you may notice a big revenue number on the right side. How important is the right side of this baseline table to you?

There is a huge difference between deciding to leave the familiar and being committed to leaving the familiar. This is the difference between awareness and action. Planning and stepping out. For most people, this is the reason you picked up this book, or hired a coach, or decided to jump into Passionate Action success. You are ready for the next step.

If you don't set a baseline standard for what you'll accept in your life, then it will be easy to slip into behaviors or attitudes or a quality of life that is far below what you deserve. You set the baseline. Then you stretch into the desired goals. Only when you leap for the stars or clouds will you step higher. In *Awaken the Giant Within*, Anthony Robbins describes the importance of a baseline when making decisions.

Did you know that the word decision means to cut away from the familiar?

What are you deciding to do right now?

Your answer to that question determines how, or if, you experience passionate action. The key phrase is "deciding to do." If you decide that you are capable of moving toward your action-based goals, then you will do so. The three most important decisions that will determine your success are:

1. Your decisions about what to focus on
2. Your decisions about what things mean to you
3. Your decisions about what to do to create the
   results you desire.

Think about those three questions and, for a second time, look back at your baseline table. Now edit your baseline based on your decisions.

I recently met a financial planner who pointed out that time is our only fixed commodity. Every other aspect of our life will vary—heath, money, relationships, careers. He repeatedly asked, "How are you deciding to use your time right now?"

Notice the difference between the following lists of questions, and how you respond to each of them.

What do you focus on?

_____

_____

_____

What do you decide to focus on?

_____

_____

_____

What is meaningful?

_____

_____

_____

What do you decide is meaningful?

_____

_____

_____

What results are you creating?

_____

_____

_____

What results are you deciding to create?

_____

_____

_____

If you are not in control, or think you are falling over Niagara Falls, you could look upstream and determine the decisions that brought you to that whitewater. Or you could look at your baseline table and make decisions about your next Passionate Action goal. It is how you make decisions, how you spend your time, not the current reality or conditions of your life that defines your success.

ACTION PLANS

Action plans are the guidelines that make your decisions and goals possible. They turn your best intentions into conscious steps. Action plans can be in many formats. In fact, the baseline that you just completed can be used on a weekly or quarterly basis to create accountability. The main point is to write it down and do it! Action plans will help you define and reach your goals. Every goal is a vision with a deadline.

My favorite anecdote about goal setting refers to a recent study of Harvard University graduates on commencement day. They were asked, "Do you have a written goal?" A scant 10% said yes. When asked, "Do you know where your written goals are located?", only 3% of them said yes. When surveyed 20 years later

"Who are you?" said the Caterpillar. Alice replied, rather shyly, "I – I hardly know, Sir, just at present – at least I know who I was when I got up this morning, but I think I must have been changed several times since then."

–Lewis Carroll

and asked a battery of questions about life satisfaction and career success, the group that had written their goals by commencement day outranked their classmates on all measures of success. And the very highest ranking group? You guessed it: those who had written their goals and could locate them in their purse or wallet. Take a moment to write your goals!

Many of my clients create action plans and post them on their mirror or in their office. My goals are taped to the wall above my computer. Where are your written goals?

The following two action plan formats are easy to use. Select one and complete it now.

Your action plan will help you, like any map, as you leave the familiar.

ACTION PLAN WORKSHEET #1—STEP ONE

Action plans help you focus.

Step One: Select one (or more) of the following areas for improvement/change:

Listening	Delegating
Time management	Communicating
Decision Making	Disciplining
Evaluating Performance	Career goals
Educational goals	Personal goals
Social goals	Motivating others
Developing people	Family goals
	Others…?

One area I choose for change or improvement:

_____

Step Two: (Next Page)
1. Set a SMART (Specific, Measurable, Attainable, Realistic, Time-Bound) goal.
2. Determine resources.
3. Commit with another person to help monitor each other's progress.
4. Decide how you will be accountable.
5. Reward yourself for making that change or improvement.

ACTION PLAN WORKSHEET #1—STEP TWO

- -

Writing commitments help us remember.

1. My SMART goal is (for example: I will be a better listener because I will pause at least three seconds after each
speaker finishes, then reflect and collect my thoughts before
sharing them, using appreciative language).

_____

_____

_____

2. Resources to support me (who, what, where available?)

_____

_____

3. Commitments: I commit to help _____
monitor his/her area for improvements/ change. I ask
_____ to commit to helping me with my
areas for improvements/change.

4. I will be accountable to my improvement or change by:

_____

5. I reward myself for completing this improvement or
change by:

_____

_____

ACTION PLAN WORKSHEET #2

Writing commitments help us remember.

Commitments I Make Now to Improve

_____

_____

_____

_____

I Choose to Start…

_____

_____

I Choose to Stop…

_____

_____

I Am Open to Changing…

_____

_____

_____

QUADRANT MODELS

One objective of this chapter is to provide you with models that can help you move from awareness to action. The final model in this chapter uses a four-quadrant box. Start by asking an either/or question. Then ask a second either/or question. Put one question on the top of the box and one question on the side of the box.

Here is an example that will help you understand your motivation. Focus on one aspect of your current life or work.

After filling in the chart to the right answer these useful questions:

1. If you were to spend at least 60% of your time doing those tasks on the left side of the quadrant, how would your life be different? List those actions and feelings.

_____

_____

_____

_____

_____

2. If you were to spend at least 60% of your time doing those tasks on the top half of the quadrant, how would your life be different? List those actions and feelings.

_____

_____

_____

_____

_____

	TASKS I LIKE	TASKS I DISLIKE
TASKS I DO WELL		
	Percentage of time spent here_____	Percentage of time spent here_____
TASKS I DO NOT DO WELL		
	Percentage of time spent here_____	Percentage of time spent here_____

Here is a second example that uses a quadrant model. If time management and goal setting are challenges for you, or if procrastination is an overwhelming current reality, you may appreciate the organizing systems described by Stephen Covey in *The Seven Habits of Highly Effective People*. He urges you to separate those activities that are urgent from those that are not urgent, then separate those that are important from those that are not important.

The upper left quadrant (QI) represents those activities that are both urgent and important. These may be the activities that push and pull you away from your Passionate Action goals. The upper right quadrant (QII) represents those activities that are important but not urgent, such as recognizing new opportunities, planning, and recreation. QI and QII are the realms of passionate action!

You will see other quadrant models in subsequent chapters because they are simple, useful, and effective. They build awareness in a quick, fun way.

After filling in the chart to the right answer these useful questions:

1. If you were to spend at least 60% of your time doing those tasks on the left side of the quadrant, how would your life be different? List those actions and feelings.

_____

_____

_____

2. If you were to spend at least 60% of your time doing those tasks on the top half of the quadrant, how would your life be different? List those actions and feelings.

_____

_____

_____

	URGENT	NOT URGENT
IMPORTANT	I	II
	Percentage of time spent here_____	Percentage of time spent here_____
NOT IMPORTANT	III	IV
	Percentage of time spent here_____	Percentage of time spent here_____

TAKING THOSE BIG STEPS

When a child learns to walk, we applaud any steps. Children are encouraged to flop around on wobbly legs, eventually stand, then take bigger and bigger steps. Suddenly the safety barriers are down and those steps become confident strides into the next room, then leaps and runs from the neighborhood into the world. Those are gigantic steps, proportionately the biggest steps our bodies ever make. As adults, we tend to take smaller steps.

What would be a big step for you? What would be an outrageous success goal?

Can you imagine traveling to the most remote corners of the world and asking people, "What is the meaning of life?" How do you think those people would reply? How would you reply?

Cultural anthropologist and mountaineer Jeff Salz did just that and described their responses in *The Way of Adventure*. He asked hundreds of people, "What is the meaning of life?"

His conclusion was, "Work. Not work defined as 'that thing we do to earn the money to get the material possessions we want that will ultimately make us happy,' but work as defined by Kahlil Gibran, the Lebanese poet and mystic, who said that work is 'love made visible.' The question for you, and anyone committed to a passionate life, is how do I change everyday work from the first kind to the second kind?

Assume for a minute that you are ready to take those bigger steps toward leaving the familiar. Then ask yourself these questions:

What is the meaning of work for you?

_____

_____

_____

_____

How would you "make love visible"?

_____

_____

_____

What would you die for?

_____

_____

_____

What would be a big step for you to take?

_____

_____

_____

How would you know if you succeeded after the big step?

_____

_____

_____

There are plenty of biographies and stories about people who have taken a big step into an adventure. For instance, Huckleberry Finn made a raft, stole off in the middle of the night down the Mississippi River, had endless challenges, and eventually returned to his town along the river. His buddy, Tom Sawyer, stayed at home. At the end of the novel, Huck said, "I reckon I got to light out for the Territory ahead of the rest...."

Just like you.

John Steinbeck loved to travel. He understood that many people have good intentions, plan forever, but never leave home. One summer he traveled around America in a camper pick-up truck with his dog, Charley. Steinbeck wrote, "A trip, a safari, an exploration, is an entity different from all other journeys. It has personality, temperament, individuality, uniqueness. A journey is like a person in itself: no two are alike. And all plans, safeguards, policing, and coercion are fruitless. We find after years of struggle that we do not take a trip; a trip takes us."

And so it is when you leave the familiar. The trip, the adventure, takes you.

CASE STUDIES

Once again, use these case studies to apply what you have just learned about the need to leave the familiar. Imagine that you are Christy or Joel.

✱ CASE STUDY A: CHRISTY

Christy is a stay-at-home mother of three school-aged children. She is physically active and restless. After some hesitation, she visited a professional coach and enjoyed the sample session. She learned some things about herself. So she invested in the coaching, and completed some forms.

The forms helped her assess some of her strengths and goals. She remembered things that were once important, but have recently been hidden from her. Each question moved like a flower petal, unfurling into something deeper, closer, more important than the last. So she completed the forms and met with her coach.

During that first session, she felt comfortable. Her coach was curious, supportive, wise enough to not say too much. She trusted the process. She walked away with specific steps in writing. And she had a process for weekly coaching sessions. Christy loved the fact that someone cared enough about her, believed in her, supported her, and would hold her accountable. Her husband supported the coaching agreement; he called it her mid-life gift to herself. So Christy agreed to meet for several months.

In the next month, Christy explored small steps away from the familiar. She completed a balance wheel. She created action plans for possible changes in her life. They included doing a short running race, maybe even a sprint triathlon, maybe starting a small business, up to 25 hours a week. She joined a group of athletes who raced and raised money to fight cancer. For the first time since she was in grade school, she started a journal.

Some questions for you include:
What is in balance in your life?

What aspects of your life are not in balance?

What are three steps you could take toward the goals on your action plan?

How would your children feel about you if you completed those steps?

What are some outrageous, big steps you could take?

How would your sense of self change if you were to leave the familiar?

✱ CASE STUDY B: JOEL

Joel is a salesman who hates phone rejection and often feels lonely. He read this chapter and did the wheel of life activity. It scared him, because he had low scores in two areas of his life that needed to be higher. His level of satisfaction with his career was a 2 out of 10, and his level of satisfaction with relationships was a 3.

Recently one of his clients asked, "How is it going?" and he paused before saying, "Just fine!" He knew that he had some work to do. His sales numbers were low. He was feeling lonely.

So he bought another copy of this book and shared it with his accountability partner at work. Karl is also on the sales team, has more seniority, and at a recent training program he was assigned to be a partner with Joel. So they completed the quadrant model together. It didn't take long to complete. They each determined what was important and listed some goals that would help their sales. Joel realized that he needed to call ten new referrals each week in order to meet with three people and sell to one person. His current call average for the past month was only six new referral calls each week. Joel knew that he needed Karl to read his daily email updates, and they agreed to meet again next week.

When Joel went home that night, his roommates had left trash in the living room. They had eaten his food in the refrigerator. Someone had written a phone message for him that was illegible. He thought about cleaning up for them. Instead, he went into his room and closed the door.

He turned to the baseline table in this chapter. He listed aspects of his personal life that were satisfactory. He looked at the time he invested into his relationship with his roommates. He looked at the money he saved by sharing the rooms. He looked at the number of dates he had in the past month. He looked at the return on each investment in his personal life. And he decided that he needed to find his own apartment. He called a friend of a client who wanted to go out for dinner. She said yes, and he moved into the unfamiliar.

Some questions for you include:
What is in balance in your life?

What aspects of your life are not in balance?

What are three steps you could take toward the goals on your action plan?

How would others feel about you if you completed those steps?

What are some outrageous, big steps you could take?

How would your sense of self change if you were to leave the familiar?

What does your ideal partner look like?

What could you say to her, if you met tonight for dinner?

YOUR ACTION ITEMS ARE

1. Complete the forms and activities above.

2. Take a walk with this book in hand. Reflect on this chapter before reading ahead.

3. Jot some notes in the margin of this chapter; review it and write some notes to yourself on each page.

4. Complete your baseline table.

5. Create passionate action by experimenting for one day. Start by changing one aspect of your appearance, change your hair style or dress better for the day. Notice how you feel and how others respond to you. Become that person for a day. Notice what you like and do not like about that new appearance, that new person. Then on another day, change another aspect of your appearance. Buy new clothes and step into them, like a king or a queen. Make it a special day! Notice the feelings of discomfort or unfamiliarity or excitement.

6. Complete your action plan right now!

TRAIL MARKERS AHEAD

TRAVEL TIP

This chapter is about taking steps again and again, even when you are not sure that you are climbing the mountain. How you Confront Challenges determines how you create success. Useful qualities, as you read this chapter, include persistence, accountability, courage, humility, and playfulness. It will also be helpful for you to be active as you read. Exercise periodically. Talk about these ideas with a friend or your coach. Avoid sitting in the same place.

CHAPTER 5

(STEP THREE)

Confront Challenges

Life will have challenges. There will be adversity. You will spend years working toward a goal before finally breaking through one level. It may take years of professional and personal development before you are promoted. It may take weeks before you find the courage to say, "Yes, I commit to coaching!" It may take hundreds of failures before you create the success of your life.

For example, my friend Paul Schurke spent years preparing for the first unassisted dogsled expedition to the North Pole. It was an epic adventure and they were successful. However, shortly after returning to northern Minnesota, he said, "I needed a new goal, some other challenge to face. So I started an equipment company and started doing speaking presentations. Then I got married."

Contrast Paul's zeal for adventure with the woman I recently met at a seminar for writers. She confessed, "I come to these seminars because I like the company of other writers. I always write more after these meetings. But the stories I write are just for me. I never expect to be published or anything." I wanted to shake her shoulders and say, "Of course you can be published! Confront the challenges!" She was dabbling on the edge of her Passionate Action goal.

One of my clients is the CEO of a medical software company that is struggling for funding, even though they have several large clients and have a good name. He recently said, "Even though we have spent six years developing this product, right now we are as close as we've ever been to running out of funds. The staff team thinks we will run out of cash in five weeks. I have one funding source for $250,000 that should come through in the nick of time. I'm having a tough time controlling all the moving parts right now. The challenges never go away."

Indeed, this chapter will help you focus on how you confront your challenges. You are facing challenges, tests, and trials in your life. You always will face challenges. How you respond to those challenges will define your success. The purpose of this chapter is to help you confront challenges with more passion. Your initial questions may include: How do I deal with this crisis? How do I deal with the next crisis? What skills do I need for success?

There is a myth that learning is a well-defined, straightforward process, as if learning could be plotted on a chart, with knowledge plotted over time. As if competencies could be purchased. In reality, learning is a messy process. We fail more often than we succeed. And we learn more from our failures than we do from our successes. Like my friend Paul, once we succeed, we need to move on to the next challenge.

The messy process of learning often means muddy boots, losing the map, getting frustrated, or not listening to others. There are different types of challenges – physical, emotional, cognitive, and spiritual (described in chapter six). Those types of challenges are intertwined.

You may already know this messy image of endless challenges. You confront one challenge only to find several more ahead. They may rise like false peaks on a mountain ridge. One example is the exhausting, endless pattern in your professional life, as you respond to one challenge after another. Suddenly your prospective client has mixed interest in your services, the sales guys say

MEN WANTED FOR HAZARDOUS JOURNEY.
SMALL WAGES, BITTER COLD, LONG MONTHS OF COMPLETE
DARKNESS, CONSTANT DANGER, SAFE RETURN DOUBTFUL.
HONOR AND RECOGNITION IN CASE OF SUCCESS.

–Sir Ernest Shackleton, 1913 Antarctic explorer

that there is less demand for your product, the production people have yet one more delay, the research and development team keeps saying that they need more time. Just when you are on top of the challenges and you submit that report, the CFO demands another report with more accountability. You submit the proposal, knowing that it could be a little better if you had just a little more time.

Or, on the home front, your daughter marches out the door with her hair brushed, wearing a new black skirt and white sweater, with her clarinet in hand, and together you proudly drive to her performance. Then you arrive at the recital hall, on schedule for a recital that started 30 minutes before you thought it started. That is the moment when we learn!

How often have you said, "I'll never make that mistake again!"? Or, how often have you asked, "What have I learned that was a mistake? And how can I make certain that I never, ever do that again?" In each of these examples, there is a period of action and reflection. You may know the process of endlessly beating your head against the wall. One of the most common complaints I hear is, "I never have enough time to get anything done well." Actually, you are describing a series of four steps, called the Action Learning cycle.

THE ACTION LEARNING MODEL

The Action Learning model is a simplified view of our challenges. It is so prevalent that I have adopted it as a company name, I present it in many training programs, I use this model when structuring my day, my meetings, work assignments, and those challenges that seem overwhelming or impossible. You can adopt it, too.

Here is an example from a client who was overwhelmed by work tasks. Her day timer was stuffed with to-do lists, big and small. Her only pleasure was that moment when she scratched items off her lists. She said, "I've been to five time management workshops in the past year. I've tried a palm pilot, but I could not see the little screen. So I gave it to a friend. I've got behavioral charts everywhere, even on my refrigerator door, to monitor weight control. There simply is not enough time in the day. I cannot do everything that needs to be done! I've got too many commitments. I need two assistants, to take care of me. It's a time management problem, right?"

I explained, "Maybe so, and maybe your concerns are not a time management problem, but an energy management problem." Her energy level was so drained that she did not know where to begin. (Does this example sound familiar?) She thought that she needed to complete everything that others asked her to do. She took on challenges, and in fact was incredibly productive. She also took on the emotional stress that led to migraines. In our coaching sessions, we used the Action Learning model to study energy management in her life.

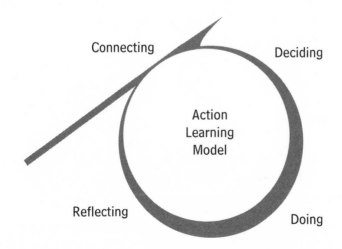

She quickly learned that the Doing portion was what she focused on. That was her immediate challenge, her frustration. To help her understand the Doing phase of the Action Learning model I asked: What is important right now? What is urgent right now? What are you doing that feels like a waste of time? What are you doing that serves your purpose? She wondered if her key challenge was somewhere else on the model.

She skipped to the Deciding phase. I asked questions such as: What are you deciding to say "yes" to? What are you deciding to say 'no' to? How does it help you when you say "no"? How does it serve the other tasks on your lists when you say "no"? How can you reward yourself when you say "no"? How do you know when saying "yes" is the right thing to do? And where in your body are you aware of the right decisions; where do you feel "body confidence"?

To help her with the Reflection phase of the Action Learning model, I asked questions like: How do you step back? When do you reflect on your challenges of the day? Where in your body do you feel the tension or stress? How many minutes per day do you practice reflection?

To help her with the Connection phase, I asked questions like: How does your office look? How does your bedroom closet look? What is connected to being busy? How does this busy pace make you feel? How long do you plan to continue this pace? How many minutes per day do you spend expressing your most important values?

And, in time, she realized where she needed to focus her energy. The greatest challenge for her was deciding to do what she wanted to do. That awareness led to exercises that helped her improve her decision-making skills.

How about you? How can you apply the Action Learning model? There are several models in this chapter; each can be applied to different challenges or different people. Think of this chapter as a tool kit that you reach into when you need to solve a problem.

PLEASURE/PAIN MOTIVATORS

Have you ever watched a child when they are hungry and want a snack, but are reluctant to ask? They may wiggle; they may cry for food, they may be aggressive.

Just like that child, people of all ages act in response to pleasure or pain. Sometimes you feel forced to move toward one challenge or another, toward one pleasure, or away from one pain. When one side of the list is heavier than the other, you move toward that side.

For example, Julie was feeling stressed about finishing some work projects before leaving for vacation. Her boss needed her to do the work. She worked hard, pushed through the deadlines, completed the project, then she became so ill that she could not travel. Her husband and children were upset and spent the week caring for her at home. She had pushed through the pain, because she anticipated the pleasure of a vacation.

Here is another example. Some 40 year old friends of mine were tired of working for others, and yearned to travel the world. They sold most of their property, paid their bills, and traveled through Central America on a jeep, then sold it and continued on mountain bikes. Eventually they flew back home. They had such a positive experience that they decided to repeat the pattern. They worked for another year, then traveled to Africa and Asia. They have now repeated this pattern for six years. We cherish their photos and emails from remote corners of the world. And they share colorful stories whenever we visit. They are so motivated by a life of pleasure and global travel, that they made it their lifestyle.

The table on page 108 shows the different motivators that may lead to change for you. Circle the questions that provoke you.

Did you know that each of us has a preference either toward pleasure or away from pain? There is some fascinating recent research that when you confront new beliefs, different portions of your brain are activated. We can isolate that portion of the brain that responds to challenges. Just like when you flex a muscle.

You may be stretching away from pain or toward pleasure.

Pain Inducing Motivators	Pleasure Enhancing Motivators
What will this cost me if I do not change?	If I make this change, how might it improve my life
What will I regret if I do not make a change?	How might this change make me feel?
How are my familiar habits limiting me physically, emotionally, mentally or spiritually?	What else could I accomplish if I made this change?
What are my beliefs preventing me from doing physically, emotionally, mentally or spiritually?	How will my friends and family feel towards me if I make this change?
What is lost if I don't make this change now?	What is gained if I make this change now?

As you review the table to the left, you may have noticed that you circled more questions on one side than the other. That is normal. Most of us are motivated by one side more than the other. Now use the questions and table below to write some notes about the challenges in your life.

What causes pain in your life?

_____

_____

_____

What will it take to reduce that pain?

_____

_____

_____

_____

What causes pleasure in your life?

_____

_____

_____

_____

What will it take to increase that pleasure?

_____

_____

_____

_____

THE GROW MODEL

When you are feeling stuck or endlessly confronting challenges, you may need a simple model to move past your blocks. Here is a simple model that works. In *Coaching for Performance*, John Whitmore states that the first step is to establish a professional relationship characterized by awareness, responsibility, and skillful questions. Then you will be ready to **GROW**, using a sequence of questions. Here is what that acronym stands for:

GOAL setting questions for short and long term goals.

REALITY checking questions to explore the current situation.

OPTIONS are open-ended questions to explore alternatives.

WHAT, WHEN, WHOM, and the WILL to commit to action.

G STANDS FOR GOAL SETTING QUESTIONS

In chapter four, leaving the familiar, you completed some action plans. Now it is time to distinguish between types of goals. Imagine a pyramid with four horizontal lines. The bottom level is process goals, the things you need to do to get what you want. The next level is performance goals, specific actions that enable you to attain certain performance levels. Performance goals are within your control, measurable, and strategic. The next level is an end goal, something that you regard as the top of the class, the finest possible, possibly beyond your control. The top level is a dream goal, something that is well above your expectations and a stretch, but still attainable.

Sample questions for you include:

If you only had an hour to focus on confronting your challenges, what would make that time useful to you?

What would you like to do with your life?

Often people are not clear about what is a goal, a wish, a want, or a vision. Before continuing with the **GROW** model, it is useful to define terms. Whitmore uses these clever acronyms to help you define your goals. Good goals must be:

SMART	PURE	CLEAR
Specific	Positively stated	Challenging so
Measurable	Understood by all	that they motivate
Attainable	Relevant	Legal
Realistic so that	Ethical to individ-	Environmentally
they create hope	ual values	sound
Time bound		Appropriate
		Recorded

Before moving on, you may want to review your Passionate Action goal. Then write that goal on the pyramid model.

R STANDS FOR REALITY SETTING QUESTIONS

These are the questions that explore your current situation, the data, the facts of the case. Your purpose is to describe the reality. This is a descriptive, not judgmental process. One veteran coach said, "Some clients will be slippery – great at describing a false reality. They may add spin onto spin without realizing that they are wandering from their description of what is realistically possible in a given situation. Trust your intuition and check their replies by asking about the data." You may be slippery too, when self-assessing. You may find it useful to have someone else challenge you with these questions.

What action have you taken on this so far?

What were the effects of that action?

When, specifically, did you feel or act that way?

On a scale of 1-10 with 10 high, how effective are you when...?

O STANDS FOR OPTIONS

Options are open-ended questions used to explore alternate strategies or courses of action. You may feel overwhelmed by endless challenges. You may not be able to see out of the foggy forest. If so, it will be helpful for you to adopt the phrase, "What if?" For instance, "What if I had more money for that project?" or "What if he was no longer a part of my life?" Your purpose is to generate a lengthy list of alternate strategies. It may be helpful for you to think broadly, by doing a mental puzzle that helps you think out of the box. Then you can assess multiple courses of action. Once you have defined more options, your decision-making process is based upon a review of the facts.

WE TEND TO GET WHAT WE FOCUS ON.
SO, IF WE FEAR FAILURE, WE ARE FOCUSED ON FAILURE
AND THAT IS WHAT WE GET.

THOSE WHO HAVE TO WIN, WIN A LOT.
THOSE WHO FEAR LOSING, LOSE A LOT.

Sample questions include:

What could you do?

What are some possibilities if you act this way?

What if that obstacle were not there?

Assume for a minute that you already know the answer. What would one answer be?

W STANDS FOR WILL TO ACTION

This step is a series of questions using the lists generated above. It may be the most enjoyable step in the G R O W model for you, because you will be committed to an important action step. You may use a chart to define WHAT is to be done, WHEN, by WHOM, and the WILL to commit to action. Make sure these are written down. You will have more success when you share your accountability with someone else.

Sample questions for you include:

What will you do before we meet again?

When will you do so?

Who or what resources, including time or money, do you need?

Will this plan meet your Passionate Action goals?

▲ ACTIVITY: LET'S MAKE A MOVIE

Woody Allen used to say that all of life is material for a movie. But who would want a movie of my life? This activity is playful and designed to help anyone think of their challenges in a different way. Are you ready to have a little fun?

   Imagine that your life is an action-based movie. You are the star. There is a famous director, an unlimited budget, a professional film crew, and you can cast any actors or actresses that you wish. They could be from any time in history, alive or dead, any place in the world or your imagination. Wow, huh? You are the lead role. Fill in the following statement and then say it loudly!

"I, _____, am the star in the new action movie due for release at a theater near you! This riveting tale is about the person who got the message, left familiar ground, confronted challenges, and returned better than ever before!"

Who would you cast as a supporting actor?

Who would you cast as a supporting actress?

How would they be dressed?

You can select any time or place, any setting for your movie. It may be an old castle or a corporate office or a remote island or a distant planet or something else.

What time frame would you select for your adventure movie?

What place would you select for your movie?

You know all about action movies. The lead character is strong and fearless. Think of Mel Gibson in *Braveheart* or Arnold Schwarzenegger in *Terminator*. Think of Angelina Jolie in *Tomb Raider* or Susan Sarandan in *Thelma and Louise*. Think of Denzel Washington in *Remember the Titans*.

You can select any super powers, strengths, or gifts. This will enable you to succeed against incredible odds, against any challenge.

What are the gifts you have selected?

What does your action hero/self look like?

What can your action hero/self do that others cannot do?

When you ask teenagers about the movies they like, they become animated as they describe their heroes. Some adults love action stories in video games and fantasy games such as "Avatar" because these are the action stories they would like to live. You may already spend several hours staring at your terminal, neglecting school and work responsibilities. The movies may have become your reality. Do you wonder why you are attracted to action movies? We all hope that "The Terminator" will walk away from the smoky ruin with minor scratches, that "The Gladiator" will confront his fate and declare his identity, that "James Bond" will once again kill the bad guy and charm the woman. We identify with each of these romantic characters. Their stories entertain us. Their challenges are not real, but our connection to them is real.

In what ways are you heroic?

When you imagine yourself as a heroic character in an action movie, it becomes easier to confront challenges. The challenges are still out there, yet somehow distant or objectified. Once you let your imagination play, those action heroes can conquer the challenge, then move on to the next challenge. As Batman says, "Pow! Poof!"

There is emerging evidence that many problems can be solved by the dreamlike free associations in the right side of our brain. Those associations float like movie images. Sometimes, when you take a mental break from direct problem solving, you can solve those challenges. You can solve problems when taking a shower, or singing in the car, or while playing foosball, or while imagining yourself in a movie.

BRAVE QUESTIONS

By now you have noticed that this book contains a lot of questions. In fact, self-coaching requires continual questions. That process leads to deeper understanding of the challenges that you are facing.

There is only one way to deepen your relationships with others. That is to ask the personal, gutsy questions that you may rarely ask. Then listen well. My friend, Alan Zimmerman, was a communication professor who experienced a personal tragedy and was hurting inside. He observed that none of his colleagues asked him the brave questions. They were kind, then distant to him. He realized that he wanted them to ask deeper, braver questions. Over time he developed a series of communication workshops and has tested them on audiences throughout the country. Now he has a weekly ezine that reaches over 40,000 people. He is one of the most sought-after speakers in the country.

Each category in his book, *Brave Questions*, contains 20 questions. Each brave question has five characteristics; they are designed to be open-ended, specific, courageous, provoke honesty, and be constructive. His mission is to encourage you to deepen your relationships by asking these and listening to those whom you care about.

You probably do not see yourself as others see you. Take a moment to ask some brave questions. Select a person who matters to you, someone with whom you want to deepen your relationship. Bring this book on your next long car ride.

Then ask a series of brave questions such as the following, and listen to the answers:

What are the most important commitments in your life right now?

What are you afraid to say to those who love you?

What is your least attractive feature?

What was one of your New Year's Resolutions for this year?

What would you do if you had seven years to live? Seven months? Seven days? Seven hours? Seven minutes? Seven seconds?

Brave questions help us to learn more about others, about their challenges, and about their desire to be trusted. For instance,

I recently climbed a mountain in North Carolina and began a conversation with a stranger on the summit who was about my age. As we peered down into Linville Gorge, he asked what I did for a living, was intrigued by my response, and asked me to ask him a brave question. I paused for a minute with this stranger. Then I asked, "What scares you?" His reply told me everything I needed to know about his current challenges.

LIVING WITH DISCOMFORT

In World War II, a German-born educator named Kurt Hahn noticed that those soldiers who survived hardships were in their 20's and 30's, not their teens. He wondered how to develop a training regimen that prepared young people for the rigors of life. And so he fled to England and founded Outward Bound, an international adventure program, named after a ship with hoisted sails heading out to sea. He knew that we all need challenges in order to develop our character, our selves.

Today, at this moment, there are Outward Bound students of all ages, throughout the world, in every environment or terrain that you can imagine. They are digging snow caves, slogging through swamps, trudging through deserts, testing a subway system, even sitting in conference rooms. One common thread in each of these courses is that each person must confront challenges in an unfamiliar environment.

Since 1982, I have worked for Outward Bound as an instructor and program manager. Whether we were trekking in England or Texas, paddling in Ontario or Georgia, climbing in New Hampshire or Maine, or talking in a conference room, these were powerful courses. People change when they confront challenges. The challenges of the weather, unfamiliar food and travel, plus the intensity of living closely with others can lead to profound awareness, profound changes. When you live with discomfort, you have no choice but to confront challenges.

NOW I SEE THE SECRET OF MAKING THE BEST PERSONS;
IT IS TO GROW IN THE OPEN AIR
AND TO EAT AND SLEEP WITH THE EARTH.

–Walt Whitman

One of my professors at Dartmouth College studied hardihood: the survival factor that determined who would be left standing at the end of the day. He found that hardiness is a trait that can be developed. When you live with discomfort, you focus on your needs, not the wants or desires in your life. Hardiness is also a critical measure of success throughout history. Those who survive the battles write the histories. Then over time, we build statues in their honor. We revere business leaders like Andrew Carnegie or Jack Welch, who beat the odds and built great companies. These statues and examples may encourage you to confront your challenges.

There are also nearby examples of living with discomfort. For instance, consider the recent interest in "reality" television shows. These shows attempt to depict the hardships of life in an unfamiliar environment. Take the *Survivor* television show. It starts with a number of castaways on an island, who attempt to survive against interpersonal and environmental stresses. Do you ever wonder why there are no stories about the domestic struggles of Ollie Olson in Watertown, South Dakota? Ever wonder why there are no television shows depicting the struggles of a small business owner, or the frustrations of an employee at a manufacturing plant, or the enthusiasm of salespeople at your local Home Depot, Best Buy, or Nordstrom store? Those stories are too familiar, too close to home!

You may be drawn to a good adventure story, an epic story of someone living with discomfort. Or you may talk on the phone, swapping stories, sharing your discomforts with others. Those discomforts may pale next to another person's challenges. Or those discomforts may give you confidence to embrace your challenges. What are the discomforts in your life or work?

■ PASSIONATE ACTION EXAMPLE #9

One client described the challenges of her start-up business this way:

"John had his agenda, his set of expectations. That was fine. But they were not mine. His job was to develop sales and marketing relationships with prospective clients. John was the front end guy. My primary responsibility was to organize the store. I took care of the website and developed the content. I handled inventory and the accounting details. It seemed like a clean distinction. It worked on paper.

"So we developed our material and presented it to the market. I built the website and storefront, and we were ready to process orders. Days went by, then weeks. Months went by. The orders never came. We had a boutique business. It looked good, but didn't serve many customers. Those were the external challenges.

"Internally, we drove each other crazy. John wanted the virtual and online process to look a certain way, then another way, so I changed them. He wondered why people didn't immediately find the website, then call us. I wanted him to be out there shaking hands and exchanging business cards. I wanted him speaking to local business leaders at Rotary and the Chamber of Commerce, writing articles in the local business papers, schmoozing with those who would want our services. So I pushed him. I'd say, 'Well, are you getting any leads? Where is your accountability system for appointments and presentations and client solutions? Show me your weekly data sheets.'

"We each tried to manage the other person. The boundaries fell apart. Instead of battling the market, we battled against each other. And so the business dissolved. Just like so many other relationships."

THE PIT OF DESPAIR

Too often you may keep your failures to yourself. However, each of us fails more often than we succeed. And if you tracked your failures, then shared them, you would do a better job of learning from them.

Joseph Campbell spent his lifetime studying the myths and

stories of cultures throughout the world and history. In *The Hero with a Thousand Faces*, he said that every hero in an adventure story must enter a Pit of Despair. This is the dark, wet, cold night when the hero's future is uncertain. Filled with doubts and questions, the hero may be surrounded by enemies, stranded on an island, unable to see any constructive choices. You may know this place. You may feel like you are on the edge of a cliff, as blind as King Lear, uncertain how to step. That Pit of Despair is horrible. And it is necessary.

One of my former clients said it better: "I am a serial entrepreneur. I know that there is some failure with every one of my ventures. But I am tired of failing. My vision for this project is huge. I need it to succeed. I need to make money. Something needs to change."

As you explore your challenges, you need tremendous empathy, and you may need to dig into the debris at the bottom of the well for "old bones." For example, certificates of accomplishment, gifts from vendors, letters of appreciation, names of possible mentors, list of the traits of admirable people that you want to work with, powerful objects to place on your desktop. Those bones may be useful, as swords or token reminders. Somewhere in that debris there may be useful clues or gifts. This is the realm of what Carl Jung, the noted psychologist, called the shadow side, the place where gremlins haunt us. This is the stuff that awakens us at 4:00 a.m. and will not permit sleep.

Thankfully, you will not remain in the Pit of Despair forever. There is a life energy stronger than any of us that pulls us upward, toward the light. After you fight the gremlins in the Pit of Despair, Campbell says that you will realize three principal gifts:

1. You have gained a heartier faith in life.
2. You acknowledge that you have the power to make a difference in your life and world.
3. You discover new alliances with others

WHEN YOU GET INTO A TIGHT PLACE
AND EVERYTHING GOES AGAINST YOU,
TILL IT SEEMS AS THOUGH YOU COULD NOT
HANG ON A MINUTE LONGER,
NEVER GIVE UP THEN,
FOR THAT IS JUST THE PLACE AND TIME
THAT THE TIDE WILL TURN.

–Harriet Beecher Stowe

True learning occurs when you do not return to the same Pit of Despair. Learning occurs when you gain awareness, climb out of the Pit, then move on. Yes, there will be other Pits of Despair. And they may be just as deep and dark and slippery. They may even be connected to each other.

Do you recall the quote from Teddy Roosevelt in chapter one? Here is the rest of that quotation:

"It is not the critic who counts... The credit belongs to the man in the arena...who, if he fails, at least fails while daring greatly, so that his place shall never be with those cold and timid souls who have never known neither victory nor defeat."

You may find it useful to draw your Pit of Despair. Then ask a series of questions like these:

What does it feel like to be in this pit?

How does it serve you?

What is keeping you there?

Who or what wants you to climb out of the pit?

How long have you been there?

What percentage of your day do you spend there?

What percentage of your week?

What percentage of your month?

What would your life be like if you were not in such a pit?

The Pit of Despair may also be a group experience, not only an individual one. A colleague who worked for Accenture, formerly Anderson Consulting, explained that whenever teams confront a change, they decrease productivity. They charted this "Pit of Despair" as a necessary response to change. Another example of this pit is the decreased financial performance of most companies after being acquired and merged into another company.

Some organizations, like some people, are inclined to stay in the Pit of Despair longer than needed. Given the pace of organizational change in our lives, you may be reluctant to change. That resistance is normal.

There are three reasons why people are resistant to change. You may be **unknowing, unable, or unwilling** to change. Which type of person are you? Here are some sample responses to each of these three challenges.

1. Unknowing. When you are inclined to say, "I do not know what to do next!", try saying, "Yes, I do; what are some of the options?" Once you explore a number of perspectives, then you can determine what choices are the most attractive. There will always be clouds of mystery. Your world is changing so rapidly that you cannot always wait until you have every detail figured out before you do anything. Often times you will need to follow your intuition, with incomplete data, to make the step into the unknown. In fact, successful businesses require such innovation. One definition of innovation is a breakthrough in every process. Can you imagine breaking through the challenges ahead? Your imagination can guide your knowing, it can suggest what to do next. In fact, if you listened only to your intellect, you would never have friendships, love affairs, or businesses. The data on failure rates might keep you in your shell, unwilling to confront any challenges.

2. Unable. When you are inclined to say, "I do not feel able to change!", try saying, "Yes, I can change, and I must." This book is filled with examples, models, assessments, and probing questions. You are able to develop skills and competencies so that you can be successful in new environments. Leaders and managers are able to train their people to succeed when the leader has moved on. Supervisors are able to provide employees with the technical skills as well as the critical interpersonal skills, including coaching, emotional intelligence, or empathic listening. And it may take some time before you realize that you are able to implement those changes at individual and organizational levels. One of my favorite questions is: What do you need to have (or need to do) in order to confront this challenge? Or try this reframed question: If you knew the answer, what would it be?

3. Unwilling. When you are inclined to say, "I am not willing to change!", try saying, "I understand that I am in a familiar comfort zone right now. But it takes guts to leave ruts. What am I willing to consider doing?" Your small steps will lead to big steps. There is tremendous power in the common saying: "If you want something you've never had, you've got to do something you've never done." There may be some discomfort or pain when you confront challenges. Yet there may be even more pain if you are not willing to change, if you fall behind, get overlooked or get downsized. Some useful questions include:

What do you know needs to change in your life or work?

What do you want to change?

What are you able to change?

What have you always wanted to do?

What are you willing to change?

What would be an outrageous change for you?

How would your life be different if you did these adventurous changes?

What challenge would pull you far onto an unfamiliar edge?

■ PASSIONATE ACTION EXAMPLE #10

There is so much to learn from other people's adventure challenges. Biographies instruct us. Some of my favorite biographies are about Abraham Lincoln, Mother Theresa, Winston Churchill, Colin Powell.

How familiar are you with one of the most dangerous adventure stories of our century? Sir Ernest Shackleton's legacy includes his story of potentially fatal challenges and extreme adventure. The details of his incredible story can barely be imagined. By 1914, hundreds had died in the race for the South Pole. Sir Ernest Shackleton had tried twice before, and was once within 800 miles when he turned back in order to save his comrades. For this expedition, he posted an ad, now famous, that read: "Men wanted for hazardous journey. Small wages, bitter cold, long months of complete darkness, constant danger, safe return doubtful. Honor and recognition in case of success."

Over 5000 men responded to that ad – it was an adventurous time in history.

In 1914-1916, Shackleton left England with 27 men on an expedition to the South Pole that lasted 23 months. Their expedition turned bad when their ship, the *Endurance*, was frozen into the polar ice. Five months later, their ship was crushed by the Antarctic ice pack. Shackleton and his men walked, used dogsleds, then sailed for six desperate days in 22-foot boats. They finally reached Elephant Island, the first land they had seen for 16 months. Desperate for rescue, Shackleton and five other men sailed over 800 miles through the frigid gale-ridden ocean. That 17-day sail has been ranked as one of the greatest boat journeys ever recorded. After finally landing on South Georgia Island, they realized they were on the uninhabited wrong side of the island. They were pinned down by freezing gales. So, Shackleton and two others climbed the unknown, unclimbed frozen mountains for three days before finally staggering into a whaling station and returning to humanity. They struggled against impossible odds before finally reaching safety. Every man survived.

That fact is Shackleton's legacy. Somehow, every man returned home safely from this horrible epic. What an incredible example of confronting challenges!

SHACKLETON'S EXAMPLE

Shackleton's example is useful, not only as an action story, but also as an example of key leadership principles that we can use every day. In *Leading at the Edge*, Dennis Perkins does just that. He uses Shackleton's story to define ten leadership lessons that apply today. When I had dinner with Perkins, he explained that you can apply Shackleton's story, or any story, as a guideline for passionate action. Here is one example, from the Shackleton story, for you to apply to your challenges.

There were countless times when his men expressed their doubts about survival. Above all, Shackleton was optimistic that they would return home.

1. How do you show your optimism? When selecting his crew, Shackleton sought people who could get along with each other. He would ask questions like, "What angers you and why?" or he would ask the applicant to sing a song.

2. What song would you sing for Shackleton? What song would you sing to show your beliefs?

3. What angers you? When forced to spend the winter imprisoned by the ice and confined to their ship, he understood that the sailors would take that news the harshest, because they had not expected to stay over. So Shackleton had them issued winter clothing ahead of the scientists and officers.

4. What food is necessary for your survival?

5. What food and drink is necessary for your comfort? Whenever their survival was most tenuous, he kept the most belligerent men right by his side, whether in his tent or lifeboat, to prevent friction. For instance, after the carpenter McNeish had threatened mutiny, Shackleton selected McNeish for the 16-day dangerous sail to Elephant Island.

6. How do you respond to meanness or conflicts?

7. **What kind of person do you want to help you as you confront your challenges?** When decisions were announced, he calmly informed everyone of their status and the next dangers ahead. For instance, after two months of camping on the ice floes, they were anxious to move ahead. They spent three days of slogging through knee-deep slush yet were only three miles from their original camp. And given the chaotic shifts of the ice floes, they were even farther away from the open water. So, Shackleton admitted the mistake and declared that they must sit tight and wait, letting the floes carry them north.

8. **What mistakes have you admitted?**

9. **What failures have you recently experienced?** He kept order. When forced to divide the group after sailing to Elephant Island, Shackleton selected his first mate, Frank Wild, with written instructions that could not deny that authority.

10. **How do you delegate responsibilities?**

11. **What do you do to create order?** When the *Endurance* was frozen in the ice, the men and sled dogs were restless. Everyone needed exercise, so Shackleton divided them into teams and collectively they took care of the dogs. They organized sled dog races, nourished a set of puppies, and created shows at Christmas.

12. **What do you do to keep your spirits high?**

13. **How do you respond when you feel frozen in place?**

14. **What challenges are you ready to confront?**

LEARNING FROM OUR MISTAKES

I learn a lot by studying biographies, adventure stories, meeting mentors and great leaders, and by listening to others. I learn the most when people share their mistakes.

My friend John is one of the fastest men in the country. At age 61, he is the Xterra age-group national champion, a regional triathlon age-group champion, an Ironman triathlete. He is also a man who struggles to balance training time with the challenges of owning a business and loving his wife. When we did a 36-hour adventure race together, we were lost at about 2:00 a.m. We huddled under a streetlight in rural West Virginia and tried to learn from our mistakes. It took some time. He was convinced that we needed to go one way, but I was not sure, wanting to use logic rather than his memory, which had been faulty prior to that point. Given our fatigue and stress, I tried extra hard to ask open-ended questions beginning with phrases such as, "I wonder if it is possible…." That process helped us get out of the woods. And we were more careful at the next trail intersections.

You may aim for the stars and fall short, but still land well above the clouds. If you learn from your mistakes, set your next goals higher, you can attain even more objectives. That is the reason why military groups practice an after-action meeting. Regardless of how critical the mission was, there is always something to be improved upon.

You may be interested in confronting challenges for different reasons. How high do you want to reach?

People confront challenges for four reasons. You may be seeking:

- Self-awareness,

- Performance improvement,

- Performance breakthrough, or

- Transformation.

Think of these levels as four layers of clouds that ascend to the stars. If you are seeking a performance breakthrough, then you must progress from self-awareness to performance improvement first. And there will always be challenges along the way.

One of the most dangerous adventure stories of modern time occurred on the Apollo 13 space mission. You may recall that the three astronauts had to abort their mission. They had little fuel and few resources. Using the ground crew and tremendous creativity, they struggled to sling-shot around the moon and eventually return to Earth.

If you watched the *Apollo 13* movie, you felt empathy for those in space, some emotional hook that drew you into their world. But you also probably knew the facts of the story – that they would succeed.

When the story ends in horror, we call it a tragedy, such as the Columbia space mission. We tend to believe that we learn more from success stories. But that is not what my friend Dean, who works for NASA, says: "Whenever there is a tragedy, the public and United States Congress demand to know why there was a problem. We need to learn about failures so that we can protect people's lives and investments."

Do you learn from your mistakes? As a child, you spent hours trying to balance on a bicycle. You struggled, wobbled, then cruised the neighborhood. As an adult, you have done the same thing at work and life. You have tried countless ways to manage or improve a difficult relationship. You have tried to understand your supervisor. But that person may still drive you nuts, you may drive him or her nuts, and therefore your relationship is stuck. You may shrug and mutter something like, "The school of hard knocks is the school of life." It is sometimes hard to learn from our mistakes.

Look at the statistics. Thomas Edison invented hundreds of patents that never became inventions. Abraham Lincoln lost five elections before finally being elected to a public office. 60% of small businesses fail within the first three years of operation, another 20% within the first five years. 50% of marriages in America today lead to divorce.

And there are plenty of nay-saying voices in the world. We can learn from them in hindsight. Consider these examples, then notice the sources and dates, and laugh out loud.

SOME BLASTS FROM THE PAST

"Everything that can be invented has been invented."
– Charles H. Duell, Commissioner, U.S. Office of Patents, 1899

"I think there is a world market for maybe five computers."
– Thomas Watson, chairman of IBM, 1943

"Computers in the future may weigh no more than 1.5 tons."
– Popular Mechanics, forecasting the relentless march of science, 1949

"I have traveled the length and breadth of this country and talked with the best people, and I can assure you that data processing is a fad that won't last out the year."
– The editor in charge of business books for Prentice Hall, 1957

"We don't like their sound, and guitar music is on the way out."
– Decca Recording Co. rejecting the Beatles, 1962

"There is no reason anyone would want a computer in their home."
– Ken Olson, president, chairman, and founder of Digital Equipment Corp., 1977

These were intelligent perspectives at one time, by very intelligent people. Now you may laugh at them or call them silly mistakes.

What are the beliefs you hold dear about confronting your challenges?

What are the mistakes you are making right now?

What are you learning from your mistakes?

What would your future self (see chapter three) say about your challenges?

Confronting challenges can feel like an endless process with mistake after mistake, step after step. The qualities of persistence, accountability, courage, humility, and playfulness will lead to your success. In fact, recent research into personality traits has taught us that when you adopt certain traits, such as persistence, even for a short time, then you will experience more success. Some of the most compelling research is on the trait of optimism.

OPTIMISM

Martin Seligman has spent years exploring the role of optimism. He found that optimistic people make more money, live longer, claim more satisfying lives, and advance further in their careers than pessimistic people. Optimism is a trait that describes most successful leaders. And thankfully, you can learn to be more optimistic.

In fact, Seligman noticed that over 50% of current psychological approaches are based on a critical model, one that requires finding the problem and correcting it. As Director of the American Psychological Association, he argued that psychologists need to focus on what is going well, affirming the positive, then reinforce the positive steps. In *Learned Optimism*, he found that your degree of optimism varies as you age and confront challenges in life. Thankfully, you can develop optimism over time. In *Authentic Happiness*, he states that coaches are instrumental in helping people define what is leading to positive change and what can make them happy. As a result, there are now "Authentic Happiness Coaches" who focus on signature strengths (see chapter six).

There are many ways to develop your optimism. One technique starts with listing your weekly challenges and reviewing them, preferably with your coach. Then review your beliefs about those challenges. You will find patterns. Start by looking at the labels you use. Instead of "dealing with" challenges, you could re-label them "confront" challenges. Instead of "making do with what we've got," you could re-label it "assess our resources before moving on." The result of new labels, more optimistic language, is a higher likelihood for success when confronting your challenges. For instance, instead of labeling your current reality a "struggle syndrome," what if you relabeled it a "luck attraction pattern?" If you believe that you attract luck, that optimistic view will lead to documented changes.

The bottom line is that you need optimism when confronting challenges. You need to believe that you can become the change you desire.

CASE STUDIES

Once again, use these case studies to apply what you have just learned about the need to confront challenges again and again. Imagine that you are Christy or Joel.

✱ CASE STUDY A: CHRISTY

Christy is a stay-at-home mother of three school-aged children. She is confronting several challenges.

She and her coach have developed a relationship based on trust and possibilities. He asks questions, she reflects and answers honestly. They each take notes. They used to meet directly in a coffee shop. Now she calls him. The phone-based coaching saves time for each of them and, in a strange way, it is deeper coaching. He listens for changes. She carefully expresses exactly what she feels and thinks. The result is an important part of her week. She

Somebody said that it couldn't be done,
But he with a chuckle replied
That "maybe it couldn't," but he would be one
Who wouldn't say so till he'd tried.
So he buckled right in with the trace of a grin
On his face. If he worried he hid it.
He started to sing as he tackled the thing
That couldn't be done, and he did it.

–Edgar A. Guest

is investing time and money and her dreams into confronting her challenges.

There are already some tangible returns. She has decided to register for a short triathlon in the area. When she learned that 70% of all new businesses are started by women, she joined a business networking group. She has decided to start a business. It was easy to create a logo design and select a name for her wall mural painting business. Her target clients are homeowners who are designing nurseries or a new look for their walls. She has created a view book with photos of the wall murals that she has already done for herself and her family. She wants to work only during the day when the children are in school, no more than 25 hours a week. She has met two prospective clients, but has not yet sold her services.

Christy has also created a life plan. Like a business plan, she used the G R O W model to determine what challenges are most important in her life. She still keeps a journal. Now she has added action plan charts that help her monitor each step. Her list of mistakes is long, which sometimes frustrates her. She knows that she wastes time talking with friends who do not have as much drive. But she enjoys those conversations and has learned to listen as if they are prospective clients or referrals.

Her children have commented on her new laptop. Her husband has commented on her smile and renewed sense of self.

Some questions for you include:

What challenges are holding you back right now?

How will you ask for that first sale?

What models or activities are working for you?

What qualities make it possible for you to confront challenge after challenge?

What are you learning from your mistakes?

✱ CASE STUDY B: JOEL

Joel is a salesman who is working on developing his career and his relationship goals.

In the last three months, Joel has continued to work with his accountability partner at work, Karl. There were times when each wanted to quit, but their numbers have shot through the roof and they know the reason why. They email daily updates with the number of new referrals called, the number of meetings scheduled, and the number of new clients. Joel's weekly average went from 6 to 11 new referral calls each week. He had his biggest month ever, and Karl has seen similar improvements. They used to meet every Monday to share goals for the week. Now they also meet on Friday to reinforce the week and plan ahead for the next week.

In fact, Joel was so excited about his success that he shared this book with a buddy who is also another soccer coach. Joel learned that when he reviewed the content, the models, and activities, it helped him confront his challenges. In fact, one night, over a few beers, they did the "Let's Make a Movie" activity. Not only was it hilarious, but Joel made a sketch of his action hero and now keeps that sketch at his work desk, in a drawer. When he makes his referral calls, he looks at the sketch and feels powerful.

It did not take Joel long to find a new apartment. He took more time painting and decorating. He wanted it to reflect his interests. He enrolled in a short class in interior design. He listed the pleasures that motivated him. That list included coaching soccer, eating Italian food, reading, and dancing. He signed up for a weekly dance class and met Stephanie there. They have been dating a couple of times each week. He also dropped his relationships with pessimistic people for a while. That included one of his former roommates. Joel learned that he had a lot more time in the evening.

One evening, after reading a biography and thinking about heroic people, Joel got out some paper. He wrote down his life goals (see chapter four). And he wrote down some optimistic scripts that reflected his values. He posted them in his bathroom. Each day for the past month, he read them aloud. And over time, he began to feel the optimism. He still has challenges every day. But these scripts and models are helping him confront the challenges.

Some questions for you include:

What challenges are holding you back right now?

How will you know when you are successful?

What models or activities are working for you?

What qualities make it possible for you to confront daily challenges?

What are you learning from your mistakes?

YOUR ACTION ITEMS ARE

1. Select one challenge in your life. List it here:

   _____

2. Select one of the models in this chapter and apply it to that challenge. Use the Action Learning model, pleasure/pain motivators, **GROW** model, brave questions, or Shackleton's adventure model. Share your notes with a friend or with your coach

3. Make an action movie of your life and that one challenge.

4. Exercise at least three times a week for at least 30 minutes.

5. Talk about some aspect of this chapter, or confronting your challenge, with your coach or a good listener.

6. Sit in a different place every day.

TRAIL MARKERS AHEAD

TRAVEL TIP

This chapter is about recognizing and applying your many gifts. As you read this chapter, adopt the belief that you have many gifts. Then you can explore physical, emotional, cognitive, or spiritual ways to share your gifts. This chapter answers the ancient question, "Why climb the mountain?" You climb not only because it is there, but also because you can return with many gifts.

CHAPTER 6

STEP FOUR

Return with a Gift

When I arrive on a summit, I love to raise my arms and dance a little jig. Whenever I close a big sale, I do the same thing. One of my clients celebrates with "the money dance," and now others in the office do so, too. Some companies have performance incentives: When they exceed expectations, everyone gets some money or a celebration reward. Have you ever noticed what happens when you give someone at work a high five? Everyone smiles and feels good. They pass along the high five to someone else. Celebration is infectious.

I start some team building training programs by encouraging people to boast a little. I ask them to share a personal or professional success for two to three minutes. Can you guess what happens? After some foot shuffling and smirking, people leap into it. You may enjoy celebrating your successes, even boasting a little bit, even if doing so is a new or uncomfortable experience.

In your busy life you may not take enough time to celebrate successes. You may not always be recognized for them. Consequently, you may learn to keep silent about your successes.

However, we need to celebrate in order to mark the transitions and changes in our lives and our work. *In Managing Transition:*

Making the Most of Change, William Bridges explains that we need to celebrate specific events in our lives. He starts with a distinction between changes and transitions. He defines changes as the external events in our lives, such as a new job or a move. And he defines transitions as the internal psychological response to that change.

There are three phases to recognizing transitions. You need to recognize: 1. What is ending, 2. What is chaotic, unknown, or in the middle zone of uncertainty, and 3. What is a new beginning. He says that most of us are functioning in that second phase, the zone of uncertainty, most of the time, and that we are running in "transition deficit." Bridges encourages us to create rituals to recognize when we are in transition, so that you can celebrate moving from one change to the next.

Think of the examples of rituals in your life: birthday parties, corporate picnics, graduations, holiday family gatherings, New Year celebrations, bar/bat mitzvahs, baptisms, retirement parties, weddings, or new product launches. Each of these celebrations marked the end of one phase and the beginning of the next. Others joined in a public ritual, and they recognized that change. Another example is in the Christian scriptures when the prodigal son returned home: He was greeted with acceptance by almost everyone in the community.

Did you know that the word community means the place where one is received as a gift?

What gifts can you celebrate with your community?

Here is an example from one of my clients who values romance in her life. At least once each week, she now gives her boyfriend a gift. It may be an object, a service, or a compliment. Over time, he has learned to do the same. And she is delighted with this exchange of romantic gifts! Now they celebrate with a candlelight dinner. She said, "The wisest people in the world may not know very much, really. There is just so much to learn.

PHYSICAL EXERCISE IS NOT MERELY NECESSARY
TO THE HEALTH AND DEVELOPMENT OF THE BODY,
BUT TO BALANCE AND CORRECT INTELLECTUAL PURSUITS AS WELL.
THE RIGHT EDUCATION MUST TUNE STRINGS OF THE BODY
AND MIND TO PERFECT SPIRITUAL HARMONY.

–Plato

HE WHO KNOWS OTHERS IS LEARNED.
HE WHO KNOWS HIMSELF IS WISE.

–Lao Tzu

But the wisest people apply what they know in a new way. Then they get what they want out of life. For me, I got more romance."

The focus of this chapter is to help you understand that you have many gifts, and can share many gifts. Like every adventurer who returns from a less familiar place, now you need to determine what gifts to carry home. When you look at your Passionate Action goal, it may be clear what you are returning with. It may be wisdom, confidence, hope, trust, empathy, money, or something else. If you are not clear, you may ask, "What do I need for success?" Your answer is another example of a gift.

MOUNTAIN GIFTS

Sometimes gifts come from unexpected places. A friend or mentor may tell you what you may need for success. A client or customer may express your gift. More often, we search for gifts. That searching process is just like climbing a mountain.

When climbing a large mountain, I experience every possible emotion. Perhaps you do too. In base camp at low elevation, I feel anticipation, then I feel the drudgery of slogging through timeless expedition days, then I feel excitement or hopefulness, and then joy on the summit. Those different feelings keep me on the edge. I may prepare the equipment, determine our schedule, select the expedition team, and move into the wilderness. There are thousands of details that contribute to our success, hundreds of people who make the summit bid possible. However, only a few people can reach the summit. Most of us prepare for the strongest among us, for that summit team, to reach a goal. We are wise enough to know the truth: There are old mountaineers. And there are bold mountaineers. But there are very few old, bold mountaineers.

That adage reflects the fact that passion alone will not lead to success. I have rescued injured climbers. I have had friends get injured or die while climbing. And I have several grey-haired mentors who have shared their wisdom.

One of my mentors, Jed Williamson, has summitted many Himalayan peaks. He also knows the dangers. I recall him saying, "Climbing is a matter of changing your perspective. Seeing life from a heightened perspective or lofty ridge has nothing to do with altitude, but everything to do with attitude. The greatest climbers in the world respect the mountains and express thanks to their support teams."

When searching for your gift, useful attitudes include humility, curiosity, openness, thankfulness, helpfulness, and acceptance. Those attitudes can be applied to any action goal, or any mountain in your life.

Climbing mountains is more than a physical pursuit. Ultimately, climbing is a metaphor for journeying toward spiritual intelligence, while deeply exploring your self physically, emotionally, and cognitively. The challenges may start out as a physical endeavor. Then you will always become emotionally and cognitively involved. Your success will depend upon your spiritual commitment. Imagine four levels to a mountain: Imagine that you are climbing from the physical to the emotional to the cognitive to the spiritual. You will experience gifts at many points along your journey, in different forms and different times.

FOUR DOMAINS/ GIFTS/ TYPES OF INTELLIGENCE: PHYSICAL, EMOTIONAL, COGNITIVE, SPIRITUAL

These four types of gifts correspond to recent research in multiple intelligence. (Some of the following content was developed with my colleagues and former business partners Lloyd Raines and Diane Hetherington.) Let me explain by defining terms.

Physical intelligence: the effective use of internal and external sensations to express your self in a healthy manner.

Emotional intelligence: the capacity to maintain awareness of the full range of your emotions, to gain insight from those emotions, and to be intentional in the constructive expression of them.

Cognitive intelligence: the mental capacity for understanding and expressing the logical systems of life and its processes.

Spiritual intelligence: the awareness, appreciation, and connection to something larger than yourself.

As individual organisms, we each developed in that same order: physically, then emotionally, then cognitively, then spiritually. As a species, Homo sapiens evolved in that same order: from physical to spiritual organisms. Our bodies developed in that order: from the oldest part of our brain at the stem, then our limbic system, then our cerebral cortex, then an area currently described as the "God Spot" in our brain. These four types of intelligence correspond to four types of gifts and define the backbone for this chapter.

Consider an example from your life. Recall a time when you had a peak experience. It could be any aspect of your personal or professional life. Physically, you were engaged, active, physiologically capable. Emotionally, you were feeling what you needed; perhaps you were full of enthusiasm, or excited about the challenges. Cognitively, you were intellectually alert and confident. Spiritually, you were committed to the belief that you could complete the mission. Your peak experience was memorable. It may still remain in vivid color! Like so many streams running downhill from a glacier, think of these as four ways to describe the passionate actions in your life. Each type is a gift.

To get started, take the Passionate Action assessment inventory in the appendix. It will quickly help you determine if you have a need for attention on the physical, emotional, cognitive, or spiritual aspects of your life. The assessment inventory is your map. It will help you determine what gifts you have, and what gifts you need to develop.

If you are a kinesthetic person, the best way to understand these four types of gifts may be to focus on your reactions, not your actions. Consider these common reactions. Circle the ones that you experience regularly.

Physically:

■ Increased heart rate

■ Increased skin temperature

■ Opened eyes, with focused pupils

■ Enervated muscles, filled with hormones

■ Alert body, prepared for flight, fright, or to freeze

Emotionally:

■ Seek associated feelings (ranging from confusion to excitement)

■ Engage familiar neuronal patterns

■ Access your values and signature strengths

■ Express the emotions that reinforce your beliefs

Cognitively:

■ Re-experience similar memories

■ Seek associations from past data

■ Consider options and outcomes

■ Analyze risks and rewards

■ Decide what reinforces your beliefs and values

■ Seek allies or resources

Spiritually:

- Explore your beliefs

- Greet your divine self or divine source

- Gain faith in the life source

- Re-define your authenticity

- Re-define your purpose in work and life

After you circled the reactions that you experience regularly, then compare them to the results of your Passionate Action assessment inventory. Your reactions are usually representative of your gifts. For instance, if you regularly experience the physical reactions listed above, you might find that your assessment inventory results indicate that you have high physical intelligence.

You could focus on your reactions to any Passionate Action goal. Consider your reactions to any of these ideas:

- Visit the local maternity ward

- Visit a retirement center with your family

- Spend the work day organizing your office

- Buy lunch for someone you want to know

- Give flowers or compliments to a stranger.

When you focus on the reaction you want to have, it may flip your perspective around. For instance, if you want to experience the gift of connection to others, you could focus on your reaction to the above five ideas. Did they sound easy or attractive or something else?

WE SHOULD BE CAREFUL TO GET OUT OF AN EXPERIENCE
ONLY THE WISDOM THAT IS IN IT — AND STOP THERE;
LEST WE BE LIKE THE CAT THAT SITS DOWN ON A HOT STOVE-LID.
SHE WILL NEVER SIT DOWN ON A HOT STOVE-LID AGAIN —
AND THAT IS WELL;
BUT ALSO SHE WILL NEVER SIT DOWN
ON A COLD ONE ANY MORE.

—Mark Twain

PHYSICAL ACTIONS MATTER

Our actions matter! Think of how often you hear phrases like, "Walk your talk" or "Take a stand" or "Vote with your body." These phrases remind me of what I need to do, and on good days, I do what I say I will do. Also, I hear what others say they will do, compare their words with their actions, and judge them accordingly.

For example, consider two common problems for small business owners. Managing time and managing people are expensive problems. When business owners do not have control over their calendar, they complain that they are running late, missing deadlines, or wasting time. When they do not have control of their employees, they have interpersonal conflicts, disagreements, or service delivery problems. These are the specific problems. They often need physical accountability to help them solve their problems.

Your actions matter! Your accountability systems may include phone calls, direct visits, email updates, diagnostic models, data charts – whatever you need to remain focused on "walking the talk."

Let's go back to definitions. Physical intelligence is defined as the effective use of internal and external sensations to express your self in a healthy manner. Internal sensations include hunger, thirst, the need for exercise, diet, medical care, and a genetic propensity for health. External sensations include environmental stressors, exposures, temperature, injury, or hardships. Think of your body as an organism floating or swimming in a world of stimuli. You act in certain ways to preserve your health.

Now look at your physical actions. To what extent are you responding to stimuli and expressing your self in a healthy manner?

To explain this point, consider any athlete. Most of the athletes I know have more awareness of their physical intelligence than non-athletes. Athletes know when they are out of balance or need to train. They stretch, condition their bodies, and prepare for the challenges of their sport. Sometimes they even stretch in the middle of a simple conversation! In a similar way, corporate athletes take actions to monitor the stresses of performance at work.

You monitor your internal and external sensations in order to work in a healthy, productive manner. The correlation between work stress and absenteeism, illness, obesity, and depression is well documented. In the United States alone, over half of the 550 million working days lost each year due to absenteeism are stress-related, and the cost is over $30 billion per year. On the other hand, you may also recognize those people who maintain good balance. They seem to balance work and physical stresses in a graceful way.

Athletes in some sports, like rock climbing or competitive figure skating, are awarded style points for their graceful response to internal and external stresses. What about you? Would your physical actions win style points?

My physical actions can be pretty mixed. When the children come home from school, and I am busy in my office, I do not always welcome them home. If I am on the phone we exchange notes like, "May I go out to play?" "Yes." Or, "When can we talk?" "In an hour, honey."

When I directed a non-profit organization, I had responsibility for about 120 staff. Much of the time, I flitted from person to person, sometimes without even finishing conversations. One time, I was jarred by a direct report who grabbed my arm and said, "I need to talk to you! This is the third time I've come to your office and I'm not going to go away!" He finally got my attention.

Here is an easy way to understand action-based success challenges. By using this table, Your Passionate Action Quadrant, you can look at your life from four directions. Start by placing your hand over the right side of the table so that you can focus on your self, the left side of the table. Notice that you can focus on your awareness or your actions. Then place your hand on the left side, look on the right side, and notice that you can focus on awareness of others or their actions. Each of these is a direction. Next, put your hand on the bottom of the table and focus on

YOUR PASSIONATE ACTION QUADRANTS

	SELF	OTHERS
AWARENESS	SELF AWARENESS	SOCIAL AWARENESS
ACTIONS	SELF CARE	SOCIAL CONTRIBUTION

PHYSICAL COMPETENCIES

	SELF	OTHERS
AWARENESS	**SELF AWARENESS** Internal/External Awareness Physical Appraisal Physical Esteem	**SOCIAL AWARENESS** Empathy/Compassion Physical Consciousness Understanding Physical Dynamics
ACTIONS	**SELF CARE** Internal/External Self-Care Sustaining Energy Resourcefulness	**SOCIAL CONTRIBUTION** Influence/Power Physical Service Interdependence

awareness. Notice that you can focus on self-awareness or awareness of others. Finally, put your hand on the top of the table and
focus on actions. Notice that you can focus on your actions or
those of others.

These four directions are useful when looking at any aspect of
your gifts. If you take the feedback from the assessment inventory
in the appendix, you can determine which quadrant to focus on,
the actions that matter most. It is one more way to determine the
gifts you have, or the gifts you want to develop.

Sometimes people want to pinpoint a type of gift, a specific
skill area to develop. In the next table you will see different competencies that correspond to each of the four quadrants above.
Think of them as the three most important skills to learn if you
want to develop your self in that one quadrant. In this chapter,
you will see three more tables with these specific competencies,
one table for each type of gift. Here is the table for your physical
gifts. These 16 competencies may be thought of as the gifts you
have in a certain type of physical challenges. For instance, if you
are very empathetic and compassionate, then your physical gift
may be social awareness. If you are energetic and able to keep
going, then your physical gift may be self care during stressful
periods.

So, what are your physical gifts?

WORDS MATTER

I recall having lunch at a small diner on the coast of Maine with
one of my mentors. He was still a devout Harvard man at 85
years young, and, by then, a retired professor. As we overlooked
the rugged spruce trees, the well-lined face of the waitress, and
the rubber fishing boots all around us, he leaned over and said,
"Watch this."

He turned to one of the fishermen and said, "Don't you think

WATCH YOUR THOUGHTS, THEY BECOME WORDS.

WATCH YOUR WORDS, THEY BECOME ACTIONS.

WATCH YOUR ACTIONS, THEY BECOME HABITS.

WATCH YOUR HABITS THEY BECOME CHARACTER.

WATCH YOUR CHARACTER, IT BECOMES YOUR DESTINY.

–Frank Outlaw

those lobsters are looking smaller than usual?"

"Well, now that you mention it, that's so. I hadn't noticed until now."

"And doesn't it seem that the fish in this chowder is a little smaller than usual?"

"Ayuh, now that you mention it, it does seem so."

Once the man was fully convinced that the lobster and fish were smaller than usual, my mentor looked over at me and winked. I was the audience, never introduced. That wink led to a sea change in the fisherman. Over time, my mentor repeatedly pointed out examples of ways that the lobster and fish were, in fact, larger than usual. Eventually the local fisherman – who was an expert on this subject – nodded and admitted "yes, yes" to the opposite perspective.

Then the retired professor turned back to me and said, "Well, there you have it, don't you? What did you just learn?"

I was appalled and unable to speak for a minute. I stated that the fisherman was easily swayed by the professor's glib words. Yet the fisherman was intelligent and capable. I know, now, the power of words. We are each easily swayed by the glib words around us. We need to listen to the still, silent voice within us that defines our truth.

Our words result from our beliefs. If you say, "I don't care" at least six times, then you will not care. Our beliefs result from our assumptions, loose generalizations, untested memories. They may be accurate assessments or they may be misinterpretations about the past. However, once we adopt a belief, we tend to forget that it is merely a belief, not the reality. Beliefs can be altered. The best way to monitor our beliefs is to control our speech.

Words have tremendous power. You closed this book or opened it again when something provoked you. You know the truth in the phrase, "Words can kill." Examples abound in our daily news, and the lives of politicians, gossips, military leaders, within each of us.

One way to be more effective is to practice using crisp language. Most of us use the same words over and again. Did you know that the average person's working vocabulary ranges between 2,000 and 10,000 words? However, there are at least 500,000 words in the English language. So, the average person only uses less than 2% of the English language. In contrast, William Shakespeare used over 24,000 words and invented over 5,000 words to use only once. And there were fewer words in use 400 years ago! You can develop your vocabulary and learn to speak with acumen.

You can also be selective about the words you use. There are at least 3,000 words that describe emotional states. Only 30% of those words describe positive emotional states. Therefore, 70% describe negative emotional states. (And some people wonder why negative emotional memories linger with us longer?) The words you select shape your beliefs and impact your actions.

Most often we repeat vocabulary and linguistic patterns. Fragments jar us. Right? If you were to change your habitual vocabulary – the words you consistently use to describe your emotional state – you would consistently change how you think, feel, and live.

One person may be happy. Another person in the same situation may be gleeful. What is the difference? The words they each chose defined the reality of that experience. By carefully selecting the exact word for the emotion, you can control the emotional beliefs you develop about that experience. For instance, when you are about to lose control, you could explode. Or you could say, "I am tired and a little peeved. Can't we resolve this problem right now?" Try this mini-adventure: Use the word gleeful in the next 24 hours and notice its effect on others.

Words reflect cultural beliefs: The English language has more verbs than nouns, reflecting our value of adventure. The Chinese language has more nouns than verbs, reflecting their value of tradition. What about your life? Are you living with more verbs or more nouns?

WITHOUT KNOWING THE FORCE OF WORDS,
IT WOULD BE IMPOSSIBLE TO KNOW MEN.

–Confucius

USING THE COMMUNICATION WHEEL

With practice, you can control your speech patterns. Can you imagine practicing five steps of a communication wheel that would help you manage conflicts, negotiate results, and state your points with clarity? The best model I have ever seen was developed by my colleague Lloyd Raines in his work at the Georgetown University coaching program. This is incredibly powerful, simple, and useful. I urge you to practice it, then master it.

▲ ACTIVITY: THE COMMUNICATION WHEEL

Full communication requires that you incorporate each of these five steps. When I have used these five concept words – data, judgment, emotion, wants, and will – I have had tremendous results. This model can be tremendously useful for you.

There are many applications of the communication wheel. Here are two examples. As you read or speak these, imagine how it would affect those who heard it. The first example uses the communication wheel for constructive feedback:

"John, may I have a minute? In our department meeting yesterday, I noticed that you became quiet when we talked about your project (data). We have been working on this project for six months. You are the project team leader. We recently secured new funding. Most of the time you set the agenda and lead the conversation. When you became quiet I wondered if you were retreating from the discussion (judgment). I felt disappointed (emotions). I want to hear from you, especially when others are discussing an area of your expertise (wants). In the future, I will ask you to speak up before we move on (will). Is there anything else you would like me to do next? "

Here is another example, using the communication wheel for the clearing of an unsettled issue:

"Paul, may I have a minute? Last Tuesday you asked me to finish that report. I worked overtime for three days to finish it by

THE COMMUNICATION WHEEL

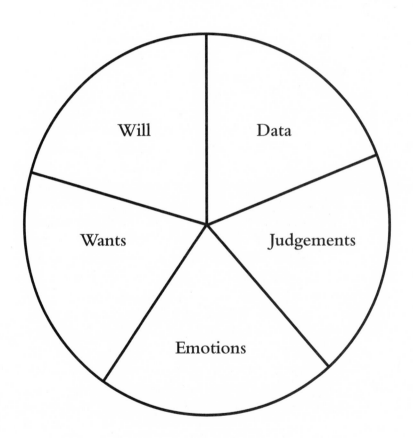

Thursday, as you requested. I sent you a digital and hard copy on Friday. Today is Tuesday and I have not heard from you (data). I believed you when you said that it was a high priority assignment (judgment). I'm frustrated and wonder if there was some miscommunication (emotions). I want to make sure we are each clear about the priority levels of future projects (wants). I am willing to do whatever it takes for us to be on the same page. My request is that you let me know if something is affecting our work relationship, or if work priorities change. I will do the same for you (wills). What would you like to do next?"

How would it feel to hear such a complete wheel? How would it feel to speak this way when needed? I encourage you to play with this model. You can use the communication wheel as a process when giving a compliment, advocating for yourself, inquiring about others, apologizing to others, as a mini-coaching framework, and/or when confirming agreements. Experiment with it and notice your effect on others.

I have also found that others can quickly learn the communication wheel. Our nine-year old recently said, "Daddy, I request that you and I play a game together after dinner and I'm willing to help with the dishes." She really gained my attention. And she used only two of the steps! Using exact language in the full communication wheel can elicit the responses you desire. Can you imagine using each step in this communication wheel to deliver a compliment?

Where can you apply this communication wheel? Start with a conversation that you want to have. Or, you may want to review a conversation that you wish had gone smoother. Then, write your ideal script, using the five key words, and practice your ideal communication by speaking aloud.

As a guideline, stay focused on 3-5 data points that lead to one related emotion, one related judgment, and one related Big Want. Then state two things you are willing to do. Start by asking "May I have two minutes of your time?" Finish by asking, "What would you like to do next?" Then use each step again and again until it becomes second nature. I am confident that you will have good results.

Data

_____

_____

_____

Judgements

_____

_____

_____

Emotions

_____

_____

_____

Wants

_____

_____

_____

Will

_____

_____

_____

EMOTIONAL GIFTS

In graduate school and my career, I have read hundreds of books on psychology. But I was astounded to learn that the best selling psychology book of all time is Daniel Goleman's *Emotional Intelligence: Why It Can Matter More than IQ*. Goleman explored the connection between emotional control and behavior. His examples ranged from individual productivity to violence in our homes and neighborhoods. Then, in *Working with Emotional Intelligence*, he focused on group expressions of an emotional quotient (E.Q.). The results are profound. Emotions determine 50-70% of the workplace climate; that climate, in turn, determines 20-30% of a company's performance. Emotional intelligence (E.I.) accounts for 85% of what distinguishes star performers in top leadership positions from low-level performers.

What if you believed that you are a star performer? Because you are reading this book, you are on the path toward emotional control and development of your self or your group.

Notice what happens when a trusted friend or mentor says, "I believe in you!" Notice how you feel right now.

Just by asking you to imagine that someone believed in you, you had an emotional response.

What you feel affects what you do. What you do affects what you feel. Feelings and actions affect each other.

Let's return to my definition. Emotional intelligence (E.I.) has three parts: awareness, insight, and expression. Emotional intelligence is defined as the capacity to maintain awareness of the full range of your emotions, to gain insight from those emotions, and to be intentional in the constructive expression of them.

How important are these three steps? Consider the business bottom line. One of my clients is a large association with an annual operating budget over $800 million. Using Goleman's research above, we learned that emotional intelligence determines 20% of that group's performance – in other words, $160 million each year. Is that number large enough to get your attention?

EMOTIONAL COMPETENCIES

	SELF	OTHERS
AWARENESS	**SELF AWARENESS** Emotional Awareness Self Esteem Self Appraisal	**SOCIAL AWARENESS** Empathy/Compassion Service Social Dynamics Understanding
ACTIONS	**SELF CARE** Emotional Expression Sustainability Inner Resourcefulness	**SOCIAL CONTRIBUTION** Influence/Power Trust Interdependence

Here is a more personal example. What do you do when your child or job is threatened? Your emotions flare, your body is physiologically charged, and you are ready to fight or scream. That process is called an amygdala hijack, and it is an ancient survival response. The amygdala is in the oldest part of your brain, at the stem. When threatened with a challenging stimulus, it triggers the limbic system and instantly sends messages to the prefrontal cortex, the front of the brain. That process is neurological and can be plotted. Think of it as the patterned response you have when that person you dislike enters the room. Whoosh! Your amygdala triggers a response that sends hormones and electrical energy throughout your body. In less than a second, your heart rate can increase 55 beats per minute. If you are resting at 100 beats per minute, then it can soar to 155 beats per minute in less than a second! This ancient survival mechanism leads to three choices: flight, freeze, or fight. Instantly, your prefrontal cortex acts like the executive center. For instance, you may have an amygdala hijack and be ready to swear out loud. Then your prefrontal cortex may caution you with a message like, "Not now, don't swear here; that's your boss!"

Thankfully, emotionally intelligence can be taught, can be learned, and can develop over time. Since 1997, I have been training people how to develop their E.I.

It may be useful for you to imagine a friendly character who could teach you some emotional intelligence. I imagine a grandmotherly figure with a twinkle in her eye, an apron, and a large wooden spoon. She reminds me to do the right thing. She cautions me to be careful with what I say.

If you recall, when discussing physical challenges, we used a table to list specific competencies. That same table can be applied to emotional, cognitive, and spiritual challenges. Each of the following competencies may be part of your gift. The competencies for emotional challenges are listed in the next table.

For instance, if you are the kind of person who others confide in or seek at social gatherings, then trust may be one of your gifts.

If you are someone who is confident of your feelings, then emotional awareness may be one of your gifts. If your assessment inventory determined that self care is an area for improvement, then developing competencies in emotional expression, sustainability, and inner resourcefulness will be helpful. You can learn to develop any of these competencies.

COGNITIVE GIFTS

You may be thinking that cognitive gifts require memorization or an intelligence test. Nothing is further from the truth.

Let's return to my definition. Cognitive intelligence is the mental capacity for understanding and expressing the logical systems of life and its processes.

The fact is that you make up your logical systems; you create order for the world. Most of the time, cognitive gifts use techniques like story telling or re-framing to understand what is going on around you. In this chapter, you will focus on two approaches that work well when self-coaching or when seeking to identify your cognitive gifts. Those techniques are called signature strengths and appreciative inquiry.

Just as you used a table to discuss physical and emotional competencies, here is the table for your specific cognitive competencies. You may begin to notice some overlap between competencies that are prevalent in several types of Passionate Action goals. One example is influence and power, another example is trust. Any of the following competencies may be one of your gifts.

These competencies are the gifts you have in a certain type of cognitive challenge. For instance, if you have a strong will and speak for what you believe is true, then you may have the gift of intellectual integrity. If you are attentive to data about your strengths and limitations regarding your knowledge, then your cognitive gift may be self-appraisal.

COGNITIVE COMPETENCIES

	SELF	OTHERS
AWARENESS	**SELF AWARENESS** Cognitive Awareness Self Respect Self Appraisal	**SOCIAL AWARENESS** Appreciation/Affinity Social Respect Social Dynamics Understanding
ACTIONS	**SELF CARE** Cognitive Expression Intellectual Integrity Inner Resourcefulness	**SOCIAL CONTRIBUTION** Influence/Power Trust Interdependence

COGNITIVE GIFTS: SIGNATURE STRENGTHS

So, what are your cognitive gifts? One way to answer that question is to focus on your strengths. For over 50 years, psychologists and therapists have focused on reducing problems associated with mental illness. Their focus has been on negative histories that determine what is neglected, or corrective histories that determine what pathology needed to be fixed. Treatment was based upon the medical science model of causality.

Martin Seligman is the leading spokesman for the new field of "positive psychology," which focuses on mental health instead of mental illness. He explains that you have a choice to develop "signature strengths" such as virtue, morality, cooperation, altruism, and goodness. These signature strengths are defined as your deeply characteristic traits. When you choose to develop these strengths, you can reach goals and lasting fulfillment.

Here is some background. Much of Seligman's early research is based on a theory called "learned helplessness." Think of a simple example, such as a rat in a maze. Classical learning theory found that animals expected a reward to follow from a stimulus, such as food after running through a maze. However, when that reward was provided randomly, the animal learned to sit passively. The fact is that cognition (such as thinking you expect a reward) does not directly result from a stimulus if it is provided randomly. That research on learned helplessness has been applied to human behavior as varied as education, parenting, and motivation benefits packages.

Seligman was troubled by research findings that forced him to revise his thinking about signature strengths. He observed that not all rats became helpless after inescapable shock. Similarly, not all people became helpless after being presented with inescapable problems or inescapable noise. In fact, 1 out of 3 people never gave up. Also, 1 out of 8 people were helpless to begin with – they wanted to give up before the experiment began. What was so distinctive about each of these groups? Clearly, their thoughts about the outcome determined their outcome.

Just as you can learn to be helpless, you can also learn to be optimistic. And we know that optimistic people live longer, healthier lives and report more life satisfaction. Optimists interpret setbacks as surmountable challenges, particular to a certain problem, or resulting from temporary circumstances or other people. Seligman's best-selling books include *Learned Optimism*, *Authentic Happiness*, and *The Optimistic Child*.

Self-help is a process based on developing signature strengths. Can you imagine developing your signature strengths so that you create a comfortable life, then a good life, then a more meaningful life? What a gift that would be.

One of my clients starts every day by reciting his signature strengths. He has written them into affirmation statements. They are posted next to his mirror, in his office, and in his briefcase. He repeats them several times each day. Over time, these statements have changed his beliefs into new actions.

Another client sings James Brown's "I Feel Good" at least once each day, regardless of the challenges. Her sales results have soared, and she has more energy during stressful periods.

So, you may be wondering, what are these signature strengths? Seligman researched across cultures and time. He determined that signature strengths:

- Have value in every culture,

- Have value in their own right, not just as a means to an end

- Are malleable – you can learn or develop these strengths.

Seligman outlined six core signature strengths. Each is listed to the right, followed by the traits associated with that signature strength. I urge you to circle those that are most important to you.

SIX CORE SIGNATURE STRENGTHS:

1. Wisdom and knowledge
Creativity (ingenuity/originality/ practical intelligence/ street smarts), Curiosity (interest in the world), Open-mindedness (judgment/critical thinking), Love of learning, Perspective (wisdom)

2. Courage
Bravery (valor), Persistence (perseverance/industry/ diligence), Integrity (genuineness/honesty), Vitality (zest/enthusiasm/energy)

3. Humanity
Love (loving and allowing oneself to be loved), Kindness (generosity/care/compassion), Social intelligence (emotional and personal intelligence)

4. Justice
Citizenship (loyalty/teamwork), Fairness (equity/justice), Leadership

5. Temperance
Forgiveness and mercy, Humility/Modesty, Prudence (caution/ discretion), Self-regulation (self-control)

6. Transcendence
Appreciation of beauty and excellence, Gratitude, Hope (optimism/future-mindedness), Humor (playfulness), Spirituality (religiousness/faith/purpose)

You may attribute your good and bad experiences to one of these six core strengths. These strengths serve you when times are good and when times are bad. When times are good, you are drawn to at least one of these six core signature strengths. When times are bad, you may be drawn to the same strength, or to a different signature strength. These signature strengths are what get you off the couch, charging forward, into passionate action. When you feel outnumbered, one of these strengths will force you to take a stand. So, when the odds against you seem to outweigh the odds in favor, which one of these core strengths do you hold on to?

USING SIGNATURE STRENGTHS

Which of these signature strengths is your strongest?

Which of these strengths do you feel is most important for your success?

What would it take for you to develop that signature strength?

What actions demonstrate that you care about that signature strength?

Positive psychology is the backbone of the coaching profession. Coaches fully believe that individuals can develop, that your values define your choices, and that your beliefs define your actions. Positive psychology is the force behind the self-improvement section in your bookstore. And it is the reason for emerging techniques that help you develop signature skills. One of those techniques is appreciative inquiry.

COGNITIVE GIFTS: APPRECIATIVE INQUIRY

Linda is a painter who loves to go to art museums. Claude is an engineer who does not see any explicit value in art. They have been married for 23 years. Linda sees the beauty in all things, and respects the possibilities. When she looks at a piece of art, she explores it with an appreciative eye, as if there is a sculptured beauty within every chunk of marble. Claude has learned something about appreciating beauty from Linda. Claude now conducts his business meetings in a different way. He now asks, "What did you like about this meeting?" or "What did our clients say they liked about this project?"

Appreciative inquiry is an approach that focuses on what works, instead of what problem needs to be solved. Appreciative inquiry (A.I.) is a process that starts with descriptions of what is working, what successes have occurred, what qualities led to those successes, and what actions will lead to further successes. The result is a map based on your positive strengths. Appreciative inquiry has roots in art appreciation, and has been applied to all aspects of interpersonal and organizational development, from teaching to parenting to managing. You can use A.I. to focus on and nurture your strengths.

One of the best introductions to A.I. is Sue Hammond's *The Thin Book of Appreciative Inquiry*. In a recent conversation, she explained that when people read a little bit about A.I., they find applications to their work; hopefully, that will be your experience, too. As you read these eight assumptions, imagine how they apply to your cognitive gifts.

EIGHT ASSUMPTIONS OF APPRECIATIVE INQUIRY:

1. In every society, organization, or group, something works.

2. What we focus on becomes our reality.

3. Reality is created in the moment, and there are multiple realities.

4. The act of asking questions of an organization or group influences the group in some way.

5. People have more confidence and comfort to journey to the future (the unknown) when they carry forward parts of the past (the known).

6. If we carry parts of the past forward, they should be what is best about the past.

7. It is important to value differences.

8. The language we use creates our reality.

Notice if any of these assumptions tug at you. It may tug with some resistance, or tug with some resonance. Put a star next to it. That assumption is important to you for some reason; it seems logical to you. You may need to understand it more.

Recall my definition of cognitive intelligence for a moment. Cognitive intelligence is the mental capacity for understanding and expressing the logical systems of life and its processes.

Whether you apply the assumptions of appreciative inquiry or signature strengths, you are using your cognitive gifts. Sometimes life seems so complex that you may have difficulty understanding or expressing any part of it. Cognitive gifts help you to focus on your beliefs, the logical systems you develop, your language, your actions, and your emotions so that you can create the outcomes you desire in life and work.

SPIRITUAL GIFTS

Earlier in this chapter, I stated that climbing a mountain is ultimately a spiritual activity. As you climb, you move from the physical level to the emotional to the cognitive. In the same way, your search for passionate action may ultimately be a spiritual activity. You may be seeking a mission at work, a more purposeful life, or be "following your bliss."

Spiritual intelligence is defined as the awareness, appreciation, and connection to something larger than yourself. In your work environment, that definition may be applied to your mission. In your personal life, it may be applied to your purpose. Or it may be applied to both work and life. To paraphrase Robert Frost when he talked about splitting wood: "Our purpose in living is to unite / our avocation and our vocation / as our two eyes make one in sight."

For nine years, I worked in Quaker schools as a teacher and an administrator. Quakers are a radical group because they believe there is "that of God in everyone." If you were to adopt that belief, then it would become necessary to accept other people, all your neighbors, however diverse or different. Throughout history, Quakers have been supporters of social equality. They supported the Underground Railroad, women's right to vote, and conscientious objection to war. They believe that anyone can grow spiritually through quiet worship and service. The founder, George Fox, said, "Walk cheerfully upon the earth, and let your lives speak for themselves." Fox and his followers literally walked across England, preaching and drumming up followers. Talk about living your spiritual gifts!

How could you "let your life speak" for your spiritual beliefs? Joseph Campbell studied mythology and compared literature from cultures throughout the world. In *The Hero with a Thousand Faces*, he said that one could have an adventure in any corner of your room, by taking a few minutes for daily reflection. Campbell urged people to "follow your bliss" wherever it may lead. In fact, his work led me to the five steps of the Passionate Action Model.

There are many ways to follow your bliss. The vision quests of every North American indigenous people celebrate the strength in the four cardinal directions before sitting down to a meal, or when embracing the morning sun. Throughout America, yoga is fast becoming a more common ritual than daily prayer. Throughout the world, people are meeting with their religious leaders to explore their role in following bliss. Another popular example sweeping through protestant churches is Rick Warren's bestseller and program, *The Purpose-Driven Life: What on Earth Am I Here For?*

What does it mean for you to "follow your bliss"?

■ **PASSIONATE ACTION EXAMPLE #11**

I have always enjoyed the simplicity of running. I just grab a pair of shoes and off I go, as free as a child. Whether at a trail head or a hotel in a new city, those shoes become portable reminders that passionate action can be found in any place at any time. For me, running leads to bliss.

I have done several ultra-marathon running races. One favorite is a 50-mile run near Washington, D.C., that I have finished three times. The course leaves a small town at 6:00 a.m., and climbs a paved road for three miles to the Appalachian Trail. Then, for 16 miles, the trail follows the rocky forested ridgeline up and down the gaps where countless people died during Civil War battles. As the sun rises, I drop down in to Harpers Ferry and the confluence of the Shenandoah and Potomac Rivers. The cliffs tower on all sides, and in the morning mist it is easy to imagine snipers or 19th-century spies searching the rocks for hints of movement or a clean shot.

Then the race course turns along the Chesapeake and Ohio Canal path for a flat, monotonous marathon of 28 miles. There are food stations every 4-6 miles, yet the tedium feels endless. I would talk with other runners about anything. I'd play goal-setting mind games using my watch, like, "I'll run for 12 minutes, then walk for one minute." Images faded in and out with each tedious mile. Short thoughts. Our children in fuzzy pink blankets. After a bath. With rosy cheeks and smiles. Bundles of love. Bundles of hope. Need to keep running. Keep moving until I can rest with them.

The last eight miles are on paved roads that wind up from the river and into a town with the finish line, a red-white-and-blue medallion, hot showers, and fried chicken. By that time, my legs are rubbery, my vision is blurred, I may have hot spots or blisters on my feet, or rashes in sensitive areas. Yet, those final miles are the most important miles to me. There is nothing finer than finishing a race! That moment of completion is why I race. It is a celebration, returning with a gift. To rest after training for so long.

For me, running is a form of active meditation that leads to moments of bliss. Sometimes I adopt a simple mantra, "P-E-C-S."

For me, those letters are a reminder that energy flows from Physical to Emotional to Cognitive to Spiritual gifts. I keep moving, and with each breath I exhale a letter. Occasionally, I feel connected to everything around me. The physical, emotional, and cognitive voices are suspended. Those are moments of spiritual fulfillment.

FULFILLMENT

Victor Frankl survived the Nazi holocaust and spent years helping people define their emotional and spiritual choices. He knew more about surviving challenge than most of us can imagine. There is a gift that survivors have, and Frankl is able to describe fulfillment using a simple model.

In *Man's Search for Ultimate Meaning*, Frankl explains that most people assess their lives or work in one of two ways. The first is on a line continuum with failure at one end and success at the other. You may assess yourself by selecting an example. Then you can determine a point on this line:

Failure  Success

For many people, that line is what defines your actions and your words. You may be working toward specific goals; for instance, a career path that you believe is important or useful.

And then, there may come a time when you feel dissatisfied and want more. Your challenges may change; the purpose for your work may no longer be clear. You may be asking questions about fulfillment such as, "Is this all there is in life? What really is my purpose?" These questions are sometimes called mid-life questions, but they can occur for anyone at any age in any career or at any point in any relationship. More accurately, these are mid-success questions.

Frankl explains that in the second way, we add another line continuum: from depression to fulfillment. Visually, his model looks like this:

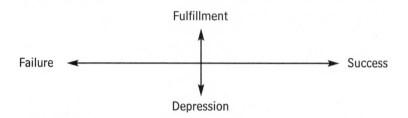

You can use this simple model to ask questions about fulfillment.

What actions are you doing that contribute toward fulfillment?

How have you spent the last 24 hours?

How would you like to spend the next 24 hours?

Notice the differences between your answers to the last two questions.

How important are those shifts to you?

How important is fulfillment to you?

Sometimes people add complexity when discussing spiritual gifts. I like to use familiar frameworks that help people determine the gifts they need. Once again, here is a table of those gifts, of your spiritual competencies.

These competencies are the gifts you have in a certain type of spiritual adventure. For instance, if you feel connected to the web of life and feel connected to a creative source larger than yourself, then you may have the gift of spiritual connection. If you take a stand and act with courage and responsibility to all forms of life, then your spiritual gift may be stewardship.

You have many gifts, and you have many ways to apply those gifts.

WE ARE WHAT WE THINK.
ALL THAT WE ARE ARISES WITH OUR THOUGHTS.
WITH OUR THOUGHTS WE MAKE THE WORLD.

–The Buddha

SPIRITUAL COMPETENCIES

	SELF	OTHERS
AWARENESS	**SELF AWARENESS** Spiritual Awareness Spiritual Connection Spiritual Self Appraisal	**SOCIAL AWARENESS** Gratitude/Compassion Global Consciousness Spiritual Dynamics Understanding
ACTIONS	**SELF CARE** Spiritual Expression Engagement & Renewal Inspiration	**SOCIAL CONTRIBUTION** Influence/Power Stewardship Interdependence

CASE STUDIES

Use these case studies to apply what you have just learned about your need to return with a gift. Imagine that you are Christy or Joel. Add your notes in the margins.

✳ CASE STUDY A: CHRISTY

Christy is still a stay-at-home mother of three school-aged children. In the last four months, she has added the challenges of running a triathlon and starting a small business.

Her professional coach is both supportive and tireless. He keeps holding her feet to the fire, and sometimes that gets too warm! Christy has noticed changes in their relationship. The best coaching sessions occur when she does not have a specific expectation or concern. When she stumbles or stutters, then they are moving into a new direction. That is the best part of their relationship, when they explore the mysterious possibilities. As time has passed, she has come to prefer phone-based coaching over the direct meetings they once had. When her office door is closed, she enjoys the privacy so much that last week she stood up and then shouted what she needed to say!

Her business has been growing. After painting four new wall mural projects, basically one each month, she celebrated with a gift for the family. She took her family skiing for the day. Everyone had a great time, especially the children, and they had a fancy dinner filled with laughter. Later, they visited a paint supplier and wrote off the day as a business expense. Christy cherishes her time spent painting wall murals, and often sings while designing beautiful murals. She has been thinking about hiring an assistant.

She shared the PECS model with her business networking group in a brief presentation. They could see the changes in her, physically and emotionally. She added examples of cognitive and spiritual changes. For the first time, she referred her coach. She also received two referrals from members of the group. Everyone seemed to know someone who wanted a wall mural painting. She smiled, full of appreciation for the quality of her work and the quality of her life. And she made it a daily goal to express thanks to people she met.

Also, she raced in her first triathlon. That was a goal she had quietly tendered for years. She felt strong, so she signed up for another.

Some questions for her, or you, include:

What did it feel like to provide the revenue for your family to celebrate for a day?

How do those you love reply when you say that you have a new client or a new wall mural project?

What do your clients say about your services?

What are the gifts in your current life?

✱ CASE STUDY B: JOEL

Salesman Joel has been developing his career and relationship goals.

At work, Joel and his accountability partner, Karl, have continued to outperform everyone else in their department. Their manager wanted to know what they have been doing. So they gave a short presentation, as a gift to their colleagues. They gave away copies of this book. Everyone did the Passionate Action Assessment Inventory and then practiced using the communication wheel with several typical work scenarios. They had fun with it and the department has seen some increased sales results.

Joel realized that he had never thought about his life as a mixture of related types of challenges. He decided to focus on his emotional challenges for a few months, especially self care. He practiced using exact diction, and listening more, when talking to others. His girlfriend, Stephanie, appreciated when he stated his feelings and expectations. He tried to associate only with positive, optimistic people. When he had no choice about it, even then he practiced using constructive language. His thoughts changed from, "What a thoughtless action" into "I wonder why that person chose to act that way?" In a journal, Joel listed the signature strengths of his closest friends and colleagues.

Then his parents visited for the weekend. They wanted to see his apartment and they were traveling nearby, so Joel had to say yes. But he felt some anxiety. They often treated him like a child. Also, not all the walls were painted, and one room was unfurnished. Part of him wanted to rush into decorating, so that they would be more comfortable. But another part of him wanted to apply the ideas from the interior decorating class into his own style. And he knew that would require more time. Shortly after his parents arrived, Joel went for a walk with them in the neighborhood. Without planning to do so, he used the communications wheel with his mom. He had written a script for the outcomes he wanted for the weekend. Those outcomes just slipped out in a natural manner during the walk. He smiled at that gift.

Some questions for him, or you, include:

What types of challenges are easier for you to address?

How did it feel to be a leader at work?

To whom have you expressed thanks or appreciation? How did those people respond to you?

What do your clients say about your services?

What are some of your gifts?

YOUR ACTION ITEMS ARE

---

1. Select one challenge in your professional or personal life. Set a goal for that challenge. Confront the challenge, using techniques from chapter five. Then celebrate your success with a friend or colleague.

2. Share a kind word or action with at least six strangers today. Notice how they respond. Notice how you feel.

3. Select an emotionally-charged conversation that you have been avoiding. Write an ideal script for that conversation, using the communication wheel. Privately practice saying the script at least ten times. Then actually use it.

4. List your signature strengths. Then re-label that list "My Gifts."

5. Take the Passionate Action inventory in the appendix. Determine your domain with the highest "Need for Attention." Is it physical, emotional, cognitive, or spiritual? Develop your gifts in that area. If you need ideas, there are 16 practices listed in the appendix.

6. Use a dictionary every day. Subscribe to an online vocabulary development program. Use words carefully.

7. Follow your bliss, whatever it may be.

TRAIL MARKERS AHEAD

TRAVEL TIP

This chapter is about determining how to serve others so that you can share your gifts with others. There are six billion people who need services of some sort. This chapter also contains examples of two services, business and parenting, and encourages you to apply the Passionate Action Model to your service calling, whatever that may be.

CHAPTER 7

Serve Others

Average people look for others to build their legacy. However, the highest achievers look within and act according to their beliefs. Dennis Kimbro explains how to act according to your beliefs in *What Makes the Great Great*. He studied the highest African-American achievers and developed a list of mental strategies that describe those maximum achievers. His list includes these nine points: 1) discover your true calling, 2) live courageously, 3) access the knowledge and creativity of your mind, 4) embrace integrity in everything you do, 5) devote yourself to work you love, 6) discover your inner worth, 7) be persistent, 8) develop spiritual awareness, and 9) leave a legacy. What a list of possible gifts!

Kimbro tells a tremendous story about a woman named Oseola McCarty, who spent her life hand-washing clothes for others in Mississippi. Despite that hard work, she always saved 50% of her small earnings. When arthritis finally prevented her from working, she was forced to retire. Her banker asked her, "So Oseola, what do you intend to do with your life savings, now that it has grown to $250,000?" She smiled and said that she had a plan. She gave 80% to the local university in the largest single gift by an African-American to a Mississippi university. Within days she rose from obscurity to celebrity. Here is how she described her life's work. "I can't do everything. But I can do something to help somebody. I don't believe that I have very much to give." Such was her modesty, and her legacy.

How do you define a successful life? Kimbro defines success as continually realizing a worthy goal or an ideal. In order for that goal to be continually realized, it must be alive and ahead, like a lofty ridgeline in the clouds. Success is subjective. Success is also attainable. Once you define that worthy goal or ideal, then you can immediately work toward it. If needed, refer back to chapter six – you have the gifts to act right now!

Adventure stories are filled with movement. However, it is not enough to have experienced wisdom. You need to share it. Buddha sat under the Bodhi tree of illumination until he attained enlightenment. Then he shared the path with others. In a moment of revelation, Mohammed was told to write the Koran for others. Climbers who summit win the bragging rights to tell stories to others.

We live in a world with six billion others. I believe that you need to share your gifts with others. If you do a Google search on "volunteer" you will find 46 million choices. Other examples may be local, such as giving blood or platelets, joining a non-profit board, helping a youth group, serving a church mission, cleaning some land, or creating a benefit event. There may be a direct or indirect return on your investment. There may be immediate benefits to your family, loved ones, or friends. Or the benefits may be less defined.

Here is an example that demonstrates service to others.

■ PASSIONATE ACTION EXAMPLE #12

The 2002 Adventure Racing National Championships were in the mountains west of Asheville, North Carolina. At checkpoint

I DON'T KNOW WHAT YOUR DESTINY WILL BE,
BUT ONE THING I KNOW:
THE ONLY ONES AMONG YOU WHO WILL BE
REALLY HAPPY ARE THOSE WHO WILL HAVE SOUGHT
AND FOUND HOW TO SERVE.

— Albert Schweitzer

THE GREAT LEADER IS SEEN AS A SERVANT FIRST —
AND THAT SIMPLE FACT IS THE KEY TO HIS GREATNESS.

–Robert Greenleaf, *Servant Leadership*

#2, we were in 6th place, our highest placing. Sometime in the late morning, while dropping down a steep trail on my mountain bike, I lost one lens from my glasses. I was the primary navigator, but could no longer read the maps. Thereafter, my teammates served as my eyes.

Later that afternoon, we were running from the climbing section through dense rhododendrons and mountain laurels. Brian became violently ill. We all wondered if he could keep going. I clipped a bungee cord from my waist to his waist and we kept running. The regular tugging gave him enough energy to continue. I served as his energizer.

At about 10:00 p.m., we could not locate the checkpoint on a mountain laced with old logging trails. We spent over an hour exploring each of them, talking about where we thought the checkpoint should be, running back and forth like scared mice in a maze. Finally, we realized that we must have plotted the checkpoint incorrectly on our map. We re-plotted, turned in that direction, found it, and raced on. We learned to focus on the objective facts, then make rational decisions together. We served as each other's cerebral cortex

When we got back to our bikes, I still had to tow Brian. We started mountain biking on fire roads, up and down. When going uphill, I could pull him forward. When going downhill, he had to grip his brakes so that he wouldn't plow into me. We served as a catalyst for each other. The team kept moving.

Sometime around midnight, we were followed by a television camera crew in a truck. Brian flirted with the photographer. We sang "Country Roads" by John Denver over and over, anything to keep our focus. As long as we thought about something else, we were able to ride fast up and down those gravel roads. We tried not to think about the bloody mess we'd create if we fell while going 40 mph downhill. The photographer served as a focus.

By 1:30 a.m., we were paddling, searching the distant shores for yellow tiki lights and the next checkpoint. Then Bill became violently ill. We had no choice but to tow our teammates. They were weak and tired, but not in great danger. We put Bill and Brian in the second canoe and towed it. Laura and I tried to stay positive; we sang every song we had ever heard. We made up lyrics to keep going and stay warm. At times, I noticed Brian or Bill with their head down, resting as we towed them, dealing with their private demons. It took 6.5 hours for us finally to complete the paddling section. Later we learned that we were one of the slowest teams on the water. We no longer felt competitive. But we finished the section. Laura and I served as the team's motor.

When back on our mountain bikes, Bill's energy – thankfully – returned. I towed Brian on the fire roads once again as the emerging daylight gave us each some energy. We biked back into the wilderness, up and down single track trails, and had to carry our bikes through the underbrush countless times. But we finished the race. We placed 15th, despite our illnesses and navigational error.

We finished because we took care of each other. Physically, emotionally, cognitively, and spiritually, we confronted the challenges, served each other, refrained from saying the wrong thing (most of the time). We returned home as good friends, committed to training together and looking ahead to other races.

Do you know the etymology of the word competition? It comes from Latin and it means to strive together.

Adventure races are not only competitions, but they are also metaphors for the work you do when you share a goal and strive to attain that goal. Consider the wise advice of anthropologist Margaret Mead about the power to impact others (see below). Consider the work you are doing right now. Who are your current teammates?

Our team felt a tremendous connection to each other, as if there were bungee cords pulling us ahead. We each served as leaders at different times. And we each served the team as followers at different times.

NEVER DOUBT THE POWER OF A SMALL GROUP OF THOUGHTFUL,
COMMITTED PEOPLE TO CHANGE THE WORLD.
INDEED, IT'S THE ONLY THING THAT EVER HAS.

–Margaret Mead

How about you? Who are you serving?

One of my colleagues is so restless that she has never held the same job for more than two years. Carla has lived in nine different states and has incredible stories about her careers in each of them. She is lovely and perpetually single; when she smiles and winks, she opens doors that others cannot open. Carla has no written goals, a disorganized home, and sometimes has trouble getting to work on time. The passion in her life is volunteer work at a neighborhood teen center. She is always on time for her work there. She stays late. She talks to kids, plays basketball, visits their homes, sends little gifts. She said, "My job is just a job. But these kids, they truly need me. I cannot imagine living anywhere else right now." She is clear that her purpose is to serve those kids.

Tennyson wrote, "to serve to strive and not to yield," when talking about passionate action. My interpretation of that line is that when I serve to strive for others' needs, and do not yield to my personal needs, then I am truly acting with passion.

SACRED ACTS

Many coaches and clergy have used Rick Warren's *The Purpose Driven Life* to define their connection to the Bible. Christian study groups have used this book to explore their faith. In similar ways, religious scholars in every faith throughout recorded history have studied the sacred words, so that they can gain understanding. Warren is using the bible as a map to help people live a more sacred, intentional life.

Think of all the sacred acts in your daily life. Prayer before a meal. Song before a sporting event. Bowing or shaking hands. A respectful pause before replying. Hand-written thank you notes. We often forget or ignore these sacred acts.

One of my mentors likes to provoke people by asking, "So, what if you were a spiritual being on a human path?" So often we think the other way around – that we are human beings on a spiritual path. Yet throughout history, the sacred acts have defined human acts.

His Holiness the Dalai Lama and Howard Cutler recently published *The Art of Happiness at Work*. Their collaboration is a study on cultures, universal truths, and what is sacred. They found that those who live with appreciation for constructive emotions describe greater happiness than those who live with destructive emotions such as anger, frustration, or lack of control. Regardless of your job title, you can learn to appreciate what is sacred. When you do so, you experience contentment, even happiness. Based on Tibetan wisdom, they describe three levels of focus in work: 1) Survival level, where you focus on salary, stability, food and clothing; 2) Career level, where you focus on advancement; and 3) Calling level, where you focus on work as a higher purpose. A powerful question related to service is, "What is your calling or purpose?"

Sacred acts are both individual and collective acts. Each one of us performs sacred acts, from yoga to prayer to your morning shower ritual. These private sacred acts enable you to move toward whatever you value. Collectively, we also create sacred acts: Football players huddle before a play, the audience creates quiet before the conductor lifts a baton, the project team has a strategic session. In fact, it may be hard to separate individual and collective acts. So often, we attribute success to individuals. Mega-star examples are abundant in sports or entertainment. Yet the wisest people know that the teams support that individual's success. When Colin Powell was appointed Chair of the Joint Chiefs, then Secretary of State, he spoke about the trust and responsibility of those who came before him, regardless of their skin color. William Shakespeare is credited as a writing genius who can communicate with different types of people. However, some research suggests that he may have signed his name to collaborative writing. When one person summits a mountain, or accepts a Nobel Prize, he or she wisely credits those who made it possible.

Quakers believe that anytime Friends gather, it is a sacred act. Imagine gathering for a scheduled Meeting for Business, Meeting for Worship, or an unscheduled visit in the hallway. Each gathering is a sacred act. Therefore, every class in a Quaker school is a sacred act. Can you imagine extending such a belief to your office or home environment?

What if every exchange you had with every person was a sacred act?

When climbers trek through the Tibetan mountains, they bow and greet others with the blessing word, Namaste. It cannot be translated, but the idea is, May the God in me embrace the God in you.

When doing performance reviews, most managers start by asking their direct report to document their year in writing, so that they can each use the data as a baseline. Then, when they meet, they can focus their conversation on performance and career goals. After walking in another person's moccasins for a while, the manager and direct reports can develop some respect and trust.

Consider the sacred acts that you make in life, in service to others or your values. One example is a commitment to marriage. You may know that married people live longer, happier lives. Why is that so? It is not logical to conclude that married people are any more optimistic than the general population, or that they started marriage any healthier than the general population. The only distinguishing characteristic is the fact that a married person is committed to something larger than oneself. The marriage requires sacrifice and compromise and service to a partner.

RESTLESSNESS

Restlessness is a common trait among those developing Passionate Action-based success. However, if your Passionate Action goal

A LEADER IS BEST WHEN PEOPLE BARELY KNOW HE EXISTS,
NOT SO GOOD WHEN PEOPLE OBEY AND ACCLAIM HIM.
WORST WHEN THEY DESPISE HIM.

"FAIL TO HONOR PEOPLE,
THEY FAIL TO HONOR YOU."
BUT OF A GOOD LEADER, WHO TALKS LITTLE
WHEN HIS WORK IS DONE, HIS AIM FULFILLED,
THE PEOPLE WILL SAY, "WE DID THIS OURSELVES.".

–Lao Tzu

includes serving others, then you will need to focus on their needs, not your own, for a while.

Perhaps like you, I have always been a restless soul. As a little boy, I ran away from home several times in the course of a week, so that I could explore the woods behind our house. I believed that from the top of a giant white pine tree, I could see the Green Mountains of Vermont. There was always another forest to explore. So I made a rope ladder and climbed the tree, hoisted up the ladder, and hid from my siblings and neighbors. Sometimes I brought a book up there.

More than most people, I have tried to purge my restlessness with outdoor adventures throughout the world. Those physical adventures were necessary, important steps. In my 20's, that passionate physical energy had to be vented, like a volcano, before I could serve others at a deeper level. In my 30's I became a teacher so that I could serve others.

When I was studying English poetry at Oxford University one summer, a lecturer scolded me, "You are so American, always searching for something else, as if the New World is a place." He was right. Restlessness is not a search for a place, but a search for contentment, a comfort within your self and with others in that place.

Some adventurers never leave their home town. Restlessness is not only a physical experience, but ultimately a spiritual one.

When Odysseus traveled from one monster to the next, from the known world to the unknown and back again, he said that he was searching for Ithaca, searching for his home. However, when he returned to Ithaca and created order, he had to journey again. Home is not only a physical or emotional place. Home is a psychological state, a slice of time when you notice fulfillment. Odysseus stayed in Ithaca as long as he could, then continued on his journey. For guidance and support, he had a wise coach, the goddess Athena, who used questions to teach him.

POWERFUL QUESTIONS

All coaches use questions to help others determine the next steps. Have you thought about questions very much?

Questions have power in three ways:

1. Questions immediately change what you are focusing on and, therefore, how you feel. Have you ever been interrupted? "Do you want to eat spaghetti tonight?" The spaghetti question jogs you, cognitively, and triggers you emotionally. It makes you shift how you feel. Boom – spaghetti – being together, wow!

2. Questions change what you delete or "forget." For instance, if you are feeling sad, and someone asks, "How are you feeling?" you may answer with sadness. But you could also recognize that you are ignoring some pleasant feelings. For instance, you may choose to say, "Things could be worse. I'm happy enough." Then suddenly you realize that you are explaining how happy you are, despite feeling sadness just moments before the question.

3. Questions change the resources available to you. Especially when you explore possibilities and ask big questions such as, "What is important to me? What do I truly value in life? What am I living in service toward?" Bigger questions lead to bigger changes.

Some questions are more powerful than others. They may elicit a long pause, or an emotional outburst. They may cause someone to cry, or blow, or pause to say, "That's a good question." I have had several clients say, "You have helped me answer questions that I have not shared with anyone, or have ignored for 25 years." Questions can also be powerful tools, like keys to an untouched closet that may help people explore their service toward others.

HE WHO ASKS QUESTIONS CANNOT AVOID THE ANSWERS.

–Cameroon proverb

DAILY POWER QUESTIONS

When athletes prepare for success, they practice daily training. When people seek changes or transformations in their life, they may practice daily prayers.

Your Passionate Action goal is defined by what you focus on. The following questions are upbeat and designed to help you focus on the positive aspects of life. You can create your own list. When answering, use free association to come up with ideas. And if you're really stuck, add the word "could" to make it easier. For instance, change the first question to: "What could make me really happy right now?" The most important aspect of this activity is to make these questions a part of your daily ritual. Try doing so for three weeks, and write your answers into a journal.

MY MORNING QUESTIONS:

What is making me really happy right now?

What am I grateful for in my life right now?

Who would appreciate hearing from me today?

What am I committed to doing in my life right now?

Who do I love right now?

MY EVENING QUESTIONS:

How have I served others today?

What did I learn today?

How has today added to the quality of my life?

Who will I thank tomorrow morning when I wake up?

Who can I help tomorrow?

One of my mentors likes to describe himself as a curmudgeon. We did some volunteer work together and, over time, he invited me to his home in New Hampshire. The wind was fierce as we sailed in a wooden boat that he had built with hundreds of his students. Then we tucked into a bay, he lowered the sails and asked, "So, how can I help you?"

I was delighted and poured out several concerns. In reflection, I learned another lesson from his question. What would happen if I asked that question ten times each day, "How can I help you?" What would happen if I followed up with those who replied? Surely my life would be filled with more service toward others.

Then my mentor asked me three questions that leveled me into action. He said: Imagine that you knew that your death was imminent, and write your answers to the following three questions:

1. **What would you do if you knew that you would die three years from now?**

_____

_____

_____

_____

_____

2. **What would you do if you knew that you would die three months from now?**

_____

_____

_____

_____

3. What would you do if you knew that you would die three days from now?

_____

_____

_____

_____

_____

LIVING WITH FLOW

You have probably watched a great basketball player rehearse before shooting a free throw. He or she will exhale, focus on the rim, slowly practice moving their arms with an imaginary ball, up and over and through the rim. The shot is all net – swoosh! You have also probably watched a great golfer take a practice swing and concentrate on a slow back swing. These athletes are creating a physical and emotional state of flow. That state enables them to succeed, while ignoring any distracting noise or movement. You can learn from them.

In Flow: The Psychology of Optimal Experience, Mihaly Csikszentmihalyi defines flow as those moments when the challenge of a task is balanced by your ability or skill. Time flows by without awareness. Our work seems effortless, fulfilling. Swoosh! Csikszentmihalyi has measured amounts of flow in different activities and in different types of people. He pioneered a technique called ESM, Experience Sampling Method. Using a pager or palm pilot, he randomly triggered responses from people during their waking hours (on average, every two hours.) Then the subjects would write down what they were doing, with whom and where, and rate emotional states, including degree of challenge, satisfaction, or frustration.

His findings are useful for you, and anyone interested in serving others. He found that people experience more flow when at work than during leisure time, and more flow when actively involved. For instance, listening to music and watching TV are passive activities that produce flow only 14% of the time, and the negative emotion of apathy 37% of the time. Games and hobbies are active and produce flow 39% of the time and apathy 17% of the time.

In an economy like ours, with surplus and relatively low unemployment, more people are choosing jobs or re-designing careers in order to produce more flow. Others are making choices based upon meaning or purpose. Career coaches have long distinguished between three types of work. You may work because it is: 1) a job that provides a paycheck, 2) a career with personal involvement and the hope of advancement, or 3) a calling or a vocation with a passionate commitment to work. Decades ago, you may have believed that only certain kinds of professions had a higher calling, such as religious leadership or Supreme Court justices. Now you may believe that all work can have a calling. The nurse who spends extra time giving a comforting word or a gentle hand is as important as the heart surgeon whose day is defined by how many operations he can complete. The low-paid teacher who measures success by how many students are able to understand a new idea is as important as the administrator who makes it possible for that teacher and student to work without interruption.

Living with flow also enables you to balance challenges and skills at an organizational and societal level. Our economy is rapidly changing from a money economy to a satisfaction economy. In contrast to the Depression days, when any job was a good job, many people are now selective about their work. You may know that money does not buy happiness. You also know that once a safety net of basic financial needs has been met, making more money has little or no effect on your well being. Money is losing power as a motivator for serving others in our capitalistic economy, especially for middle-class Americans.

Many people have applied the concept of living with flow at individual levels. In *Play to Win*, Larry and Hersch Wilson have applied their expertise as salesmen to help others understand that results are external consequences, not internal causes. They ask, "What would happen if you started with the belief that there is no such thing as failure?" What if you adopted that as a strategic belief and repeated the mantra, 'I cannot fail, I can only learn and grow'? In that case, every cold call would take you closer to your sales quota. This would be the motivating belief, the result that would help you pick up the phone again and again. After each call, you would say to yourself, 'Thank you for bringing me $20 closer to my goal.' Then you would dial the next number."

There are countless directions for you to serve others. You may want to apply ideas from this chapter to your work as an educator, health professional, or retail salesperson; you may want to apply it to your parenting or loved ones. As a business leader, or civic leader, you can apply the Passionate Action Model to developing your services. The next example can be applied to any business, yet you can apply the example to any place where you serve others.

How do you think of business? Robert Kiyosaki, in his best-selling *Rich Dad, Poor Dad* books, teaches that business is ultimately an act of generosity. The ultimate purpose of business is to serve others. The most generous business person provides products and services that create jobs for the most people. In fact, the more generous the business leader, the more prosperous the business.

CREATING YOUR SERVICE BUSINESS

One way to determine how to serve others is to select a market niche that fascinates you. There is a world of difference between marketing a service and doing the service. It's the difference between marketing a business and being in business. Although the following example is useful for those developing a coaching business, it can be applied to any business. In fact, many of my clients are financial professionals.

Your first step is to determine the what and the how – what you can do and how you can serve others. People will hire you when they trust that you can help them solve their specific problems. So, your market niche needs to have three qualities. Your niche must be: 1) some area that you are passionate about, 2) something that you are great at, or can become great at, and 3) something people want, need, and are willing to pay for.

Take a moment to list some of those three qualities. The form on the right hand page can help you determine what your service business may be. Once you complete that chart, ask yourself:

1. What stands out as a possible service business?

_____

_____

_____

_____

2. What is written in bold letters, or golden letters?

_____

_____

_____

_____

3. What could be a specific niche for me?

_____

_____

_____

_____

WHAT AM I PASSIONATE ABOUT	WHAT AM I GREAT AT	WHAT PEOPLE WANT OR NEED

Sometimes people feel discouraged after doing this activity because they notice that they have a broad niche. They may want to serve too many different types of people. Your service niche needs to be specific. For instance, my own niche is "helping business leaders get the results they desire in life and work." The more specific your niche is, then the more referrals will lead to sample sessions, contracts, revenue, and your passion shared in the world.

The second step, your marketing strategy, follows from your niche. Your strategy needs to be grounded in the numbers. Many prospective coaches believe that they need to have hundreds of clients in order to have a specific income. That is simply not the case. To determine your marketing strategy, modify this chart using the criteria you need to measure your business success.

Clients per Month	Number of Months	Revenue per Client	Revenue per Month	Revenue per Year	New Clients per Month
10	6	$400	$4000	$48,000	2
20	6	$400	$8000	$96,000	3

SOME MEN SEE THINGS AS THEY ARE AND SAY, "WHY?"
I DREAM OF THINGS THAT NEVER WERE AND SAY, "WHY NOT?"

–George Bernard Shaw

For your intended business, what numbers do you need in order to define success? Create your chart using the column headings above, or the headings you need to define your success.

Once you have determined your marketing niche and strategy, your third step is to determine the who and the what statement, your unique niche. Who do you work with and what problems do you solve? Here is an example: "I work with business leaders in transition. I help them determine the steps that will help them get the results they desire." Or, "I help busy educators find the resources they need to control students who are not reading at grade level." Or, "I help employees manage their time better by using technology that tracks their productivity and next steps."

For your service business:

- Determine your what and how statement, your marketing niche.

- Do the numbers to determine your business strategy.

- Create your who and what statement, your unique niche.

If you are having difficulty determining who to serve, then you may appreciate the following example from the coaching profession. However, I encourage you to do the due diligence in your service business field.

Imagine that you want to be a coach. You need to start by researching what and how others in the coaching profession are doing. This "what and how statement" requires some research, called due diligence, into your field of business. Here is one example. In 2002, the International Coaching Federation (ICF) conducted a study of over 2,500 coaches. They found four types of coaching niches. Those who replied "often" or "very often" to specific issues are listed below. The result is a list of what other coaches are doing.

Small business or entrepreneurial coaching
- Marketing products or services
- Increase sales and/or revenues

Corporate or executive coaching
- Management training
- Leadership development
- Team building
- Building employee morale
- Conflict management
- Creating a compelling vision
- Organizational development
- Strategic planning
- Transitions and change management

Career or transition coaching
- Career transition
- Making big career decisions
- In a corporate job or considering one
- Struggling with whether to stay in a corporate job
- Readiness to look for another career
- Values and issues of loyalty and security

Personal or life coaching
- Clarify and pursue goals
- Life vision and enhancement
- Focusing time, energy and resources
- Living a balanced life
- Values

Once you know what other coaches are doing, you can select what issues you are passionate about serving. How you serve them is up to you and is the result of your passion and strategic goals. In fact, determining your passion and creating strategic goals is a compelling reason to hire a business coach!

Creating a business is an exciting way to serve others. I have started three businesses and directed a non-profit. However, nothing prepared me for the biggest adventure of my life.

PARENTING AS A SERVICE

You may already think of parenting as an act of service. You may know how that first instant of seeing your first child changed your life forever. Or you may be so burdened by your parenting that you cannot see it as an act of service.

Just before our first child was born, one of my high-school-aged students said, "You are going to be all sleepy and grumpy in a few weeks, I can already imagine it. You're a good teacher now, but soon you'll be a great teacher. I've seen it before." She was wise, and she was right.

At that point I had more experience with adolescents than most people have. For 13 years, I had lived and worked in independent boarding schools as a teacher, coach, and dorm parent. I had led wilderness expeditions with adolescents and adults all over the world. I had great training as a surrogate parent. However, that preparation was not adequate. Perhaps you felt the same way.

Now, instead of scaling a rocky slab or going for a long run, I began to ask new questions. How important is it to me to make this dicey move on this cliff? How important is it to ski down this steep slope when the people I love are still in bed asleep? Parenting changed me in ways that I have only begun to explore.

There are many books on how to parent, and that is not the focus of this book. However, it may be useful for you to recognize that the most important adventure of your life may include new characters such as Barney, Sesame Street, Dr. Seuss, and diapers. Get the message. There may not be a great support system, especially if you are the primary parent or a stay-at-home parent. Most men do not tell their stories, or arrange to meet at a playground or library story-telling session. I can recall spending hours pushing a two-seater baby jogger through the streets and paths near our home. Training for long running races, clearing my head. Leaving the familiar. Then we'd stop at a tot lot and the children would play. Out came the sippy cups and zip-lock bags full of Cheerios. I would read or watch them, sometimes play tag with them. There were very few other men. The conversations with women, the mothers, were often awkward. Confronting the challenges. One woman even declared, "Those are not your children. They don't look at all like you!"

Parenting can be a lonely act of service. And there is no manual on how to be a great parent, although there are many books containing wisdom. Martin Seligman applied some ideas from positive psychology that may be useful to you. In *The Optimistic Child*, he lists three principles for parenting: 1) positive emotion (versus negative) broadens and builds the intellectual, social, and physical resources that your children draw upon later in life; 2) augmenting positive emotions in your children can start an upward spiral of positive emotion; 3) the positive traits that your child displays are just as real and authentic as those negative traits. You can directly apply these three principles to your work as a parent serving others.

APPLYING THE PASSIONATE ACTION MODEL

The Passionate Action Model can be applied to parenting just as it can be applied to business or any endeavor. I urge you to adopt or modify the following questions so that they are relevant to you. This example focuses on parenting; your example may not. And I urge you to doodle in the margins, have some fun with these questions. Notice where they lead you.

What is your Passionate Action goal related to parenting?

1. Get the message. What does it mean to be a parent? What are you giving up? What are you gaining? What excites you? What frightens you about parenting? How many children do you want? What if some of your children were adopted or part of a new, blended family?

2. Leave the familiar. Before parenting, what did you think would be exciting? Who are great parents that you know? What are some of their best qualities? Write these down, because these qualities represent the values that you want to demonstrate as a parent. What are some of your partner's significant strengths as a parent? What are some parenting skills your partner lacks or needs to develop? What are some of your significant strengths as a parent? What are some parenting skills that you need to develop?

3. Confront challenges. How are you going to take care of a sick child? Whose career is more important? Whose career has more potential net worth? What assets do you need ahead? How do you expect you will respond to challenges such as sleeplessness, poor health, your child's health problems, financial concern, job status, saving for the future, your home, your car, your partner, private time, personal growth, your dreams, romance, vacations, rejection, surprises, fears, and satisfaction?

4. Return with a gift. What do you want this child to become? What activities or projects would you like to do with this child at age 5, 10, 15, 20, 25, 45, 55, 65, 75? What qualities do you want this child to carry? What do you want others to say about this child? How can you appreciate the gifts of this child every day?

5. Serve others. What do you want this child to say about you? How do you want to be remembered? How do you want your child to love? What values do you want your child to share with others? How will you know if your parenting has been successful? How will you show your love for your child?

Hopefully, there will be that quiet moment, when you return home to your room and stare with adoration at this baby, at your baby. This baby is unique to the world, because it is yours. Nothing can prepare you for that private moment when you stare at the baby, and wonder. You may talk to your child, share blessings and hopes. You may be curious about small features like wrinkly hands and toes. You may be astounded at what you have produced, awed by the enormity, or horrified by the responsibility ahead. You may be gleeful and unable to control your enthusiasm. That quiet moment is the time for you to focus on how to serve your child.

Our children teach us what we need to learn.

Recently my daughter asked, "Why do you have to talk to people at night when you could be reading us a story or talking in bed? It makes me think that your work is more important than spending time with me." What a heart-breaking eye-opener! Yes, I immediately changed my client schedule. Your children may describe and define your legacy.

CASE STUDIES

Once again, use these case studies to apply what you have just learned about the need to serve others. Imagine that you are Christy or Joel.

✳ CASE STUDY A: CHRISTY

Christy is glad to be a parent. Her three school-aged children drive her batty at times, but so does her husband. In the past year, she has added the challenges of monthly triathlons and owning a small business. Her coaching relationship has developed in surprising ways.

Her professional coach still forces her to be accountable for her goals. When he refers to notes from a previous session, she cringes sometimes, knowing that he will ask about something that she had neglected. Thankfully, he also whoops with delight, celebrating when she reaches other goals. She respects and appreciates their professional boundaries. Part of her wants to stop using the services; part of her wants to keep working with her coach for years. She cannot imagine where she would be without her coach.

Her business has continued to grow. She now has two independent contractors working with her. Christy brings her view book when meeting the prospective clients, and it contains photos of the independent contractors and samples of their styles. She works like a broker, making sure that everyone is happy. She encourages every client to write a testimonial, send referrals, add a photo of their mural to her website. She has established a merchant account with local paint suppliers. She has defined a solid niche in the home design market. Framed clippings from two newspaper articles adorn her walls.

Her family recently enjoyed a weekend retreat that included something for everyone. The kids went on a chaperoned day trip. Christy spent hours at the spa, then she and her husband received deep massages. They called it their annual company retreat, and there was so much laughter that it just might become a tradition.

She gave two public seminars, plus one to those in her business networking group. Her title was, "Starting a Home-based Business," but the subject was her story. She loved every minute of it. The interactions were fun, lively, full of ideas exchanged with those in the community. Several women invited Christy to join their Business Woman's Group. She smiled at the invitation and appreciated their community involvement, helpfulness, collegiality, and confidence.

Some questions for you include:

What did it feel like to serve others in your community?

What do your clients, friends, and neighbors say about your services?

How do those you love reply when you say that you have a new client or a new independent contractor?

What will be your next Passionate Action success?

✱ CASE STUDY B: JOEL

Joel is a salesman who has been successfully developing his career and relationship goals.

For the past six months, he has continued to work with his accountability partner, Karl, on some productivity goals. He stays focused on what he calls "the small stuff," the essential details of being responsive to customers and making sure that their needs are met. His numbers have remained high. Recently, his sales manager has recognized his achievements with a bonus and a better office. Then Joel and Karl were asked to submit a proposal to present their approach at a regional sales meeting. They did so, had fun with it, enjoyed the response from others, and each realized that they are great trainers. Now, in addition to meeting their sales quota, they have decided to commit three days each month to training new hires or recruiting at nearby colleges and universities. Joel has learned that – more important than the stipend he receives from the corporate office – he loves being recognized by others as a successful leader in his field.

To date, Joel's focus has been on personal goals, not on sharing with others. He recognized his restlessness, and defined his success goals related to relationships. He applied that outline to a list of sacred acts, but nothing seemed to result for him. Then he wrote some daily power questions and read them each morning and each evening. For the first time in his life, he kept a journal. To his surprise, when he read those notes several weeks later, they disturbed him immensely. He realized that he was not living in support of some deep values, such as a desire to help others and a desire to raise a family.

He shared some of his notes with some friends, including Stephanie. At first she was uncertain how to respond. Then he explained that he wanted to define his legacy. She helped him list some ways that he could serve others. And she agreed to help him stay focused on that list.

Some questions for you include:

What did it feel like to be recognized as a leader at work?

If you lived a life in service toward others, what would that look like?

How did it feel to share some notes about what you value with your friend Stephanie?

What do your clients and colleagues say about your service toward others?

What will be your next Passionate Action success?

YOUR ACTION ITEMS ARE

----

1. Select one aspect of your life that could be an area for service. Use the Passionate Action outline in chapter two to explore how you might live a life of service.

2. Describe what your legacy could be. Use your coach or accountability partner to explore that legacy. Create the specific steps that would make your legacy happen.

3. Create your own weather. In the mountains, the weather changes instantly, and the best climbers carry some sunshine in their heart and words. Regardless of how cold and wet it is outside, share some summertime kindness with a stranger.

4. Volunteer to help others. If you are seeking ideas, ask your friends and neighbors for ideas. Watch their eyes light up as they describe their youth league coaching, church committee, neighborhood clean-up, or a favorite charity.

5. Commit to contributing at least 10% of your annual revenue to charities and non-profits. Notice how that giving affects your spirit.

6. Talk about some aspect of this chapter with an older person. Ask them what they value in life, then listen well.

TRAIL MARKERS AHEAD

TRAVEL TIP

This chapter is about organizing yourself so that you can travel with confidence, as if your map is tucked under your arm. Your future trails may be wet or overgrown at times. My hope is that there are many future trails ahead for you, and that you stride toward them.

CHAPTER 8

Future Trails

After any big adventure, I like to stand up and exhale. Don't you? Take a big breath! If needed, return to previous chapters, take a few gems and apply them to your Passionate Action goals.

When I facilitate meetings, I try to spend 10% of the time gathering strings and determining the next steps. For example, each hour-long meeting requires at least six minutes for closure. If you spent six hours reading this book, set aside one hour for review. That hour will define your future trails.

One of the most experienced trainers I ever worked with said, "Closure is all that people remember from a training program. During the training, people are mostly concerned with three things – food, fun, and friendship. Afterward, they need to put it all together. They need to move from 'So what?' to 'Now what?'"

My corporate clients ask, "Are we any smarter now when we ask the same question, 'So, where do we go from here?'" I sure hope so! By now, you should have some good material for creating extraordinary success in your life and work. Now you need to implement these five steps. You need to create a map! Imagine all the white space – all the open possibilities of an empty map....

MAP MAKING

I love looking at maps and have file folders stuffed with favorite maps. Some include places I have been, like Yosemite or the New York subway. Some include places I want to go, like the South Island of New Zealand or La Paz, Bolivia. I keep maps in the car for easy access to metropolitan areas. I keep bookmarks of online map directories. One year, I gave everyone in my family gigantic maps – 4'x3' maps for their walls or ceilings, anything to foster their dreams.

Throughout recorded time, maps have always been useful, familiar guidelines. We trust them. Now we reach for maps in our glove compartment or print out directions before leaving the office or base camp. Our cars have digital maps with GPS, Global Positioning Systems. We need to know where we are, so that we can determine where we need to go.

Maps are external references for our goals. The following image, the Passionate Action Model, is a map. This book is also a map.

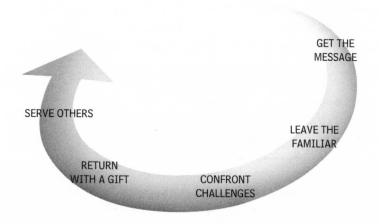

GET THE MESSAGE

SERVE OTHERS

LEAVE THE FAMILIAR

RETURN WITH A GIFT

CONFRONT CHALLENGES

Consider the sport of orienteering as a quick example. Orienteering races are designed for those who love running through unfamiliar terrain with a map and a compass. There is one master map at the start line. It is marked with orienteering points (OP's), and your task is to find them in the forest as quickly as possible. However, your first job is to copy the OP's onto your handheld map from the master map. Not only do you need to know how to read the local topographical features of boulders and ridges, but also you need to copy the OP's exactly from the master map. Many races are lost because of an error before the starting line.

Your job now is to make a map for your future success.

Your map may be colorful and it may be vague. Columbus, Magellan, Drake, and Meriwether Lewis had little idea of what territory lay ahead. So it is with your success. Maps define starting points, not ending points. Maps are useful guidelines for what we carry into the wilds, just like any three-month business plan. They are not prescriptions for safe travel. Your job is to make a map that starts with what you value or believe to be true.

MIND MAPS

How often do you watch clouds form and reform in a windy sky?

How often do you listen to conversations popping up from others in a busy restaurant? You will hear a word here, a sentence there. Your brain processes these sounds by shifting attention to one and then the next. That process is called your reticular activating system and it is what enables you to hear your loved one calling your name across the crowded movie lobby or at that noisy dinner party.

We hear and see what we attend to. There are countless examples in marketing and advertising. Radio commercials are louder than the songs. Print ads include subliminal pictures such as the sensual woman in the ice cube of whiskey. In one experiment, a movie ad included hidden images of popcorn to promote sales of popcorn. Conversely, we can block out these distracting messages when it is time to perform. Think of the athlete stepping up to bat, or yourself just before a travel deadline. You are incredibly productive.

Our brains process stimuli in an associative way, like clouds floating or bubbles popping. One idea·triggers another, then another, and we follow that wispy cloud into the horizon.

Tony Buzan, in *The Mind Map Book*, explains that we do not think in linear ways. Our brains simply do not work in an outline format with a series of sequential points like a computer program. We can learn to write outlines; that is a skill that can be developed through rigid schooling. However, we think associatively, not sequentially. And the bubbles pop and transform almost instantaneously.

Mind maps are useful techniques for brainstorming, problem solving, and decision making. They are the best technique I know for making maps.

Start with a large piece of paper, ideally a flip chart on the floor, and several bright-colored markers. Start in the center of the paper by drawing a circle or a lumpy cloud. Inside that cloud write the subject or something you value or believe to be true. That word is your starting point. Select any colored marker and ask yourself questions, beginning with "how" or "what." Then jot down the associations, whatever pops into your head, as fast as you can, while you explore in that direction. For instance, if you asked, "What would that look like?" you might select one color and define a strand of options, like bubbles or clouds in one direction. Whenever the impulse grabs you, select another colored marker, and trace another series of associations. Soon you will be filling the paper with ideas.

The product is called a mind map. It represents a series of associations, possible directions for your future success. You can create mind maps alone or in a small group. You can break down a complicated process into any step. Work teams can concurrently develop mind maps in small groups. You can start with a business challenge or an interpersonal conflict. You can time the activity and have people discuss their best idea, then report out. You can use mind maps to energize a team, even as a regular agenda item in meetings. The mind maps can be posted in your hallways or on a whiteboard.

▲ ACTIVITY: YOUR MIND MAP

Directions: Use the space below to create a mind map that explores one of your core values. Start by selecting one and writing it in the center of the page.

Your mental maps will define the course of your success. Whatever you develop will be a useful guide in the middle of the night or when you are not certain of your direction.

If you prefer to use the outline format, here is a copy from chapter two. You may have some notes in previous chapters, and they may have changed as you have thought more about your goals. If you need a map, complete this outline now.

My Passionate Action goal is to:

_____

_____

_____

My Passionate Action goal looks like this:

1. Get the message

a. _____

_____

b. _____

_____

c. _____

_____

2. Leave the familiar

a. _____

_____

b. _____

_____

c. _____

_____

3. Confront challenges

a. _____

_____

b. _____

_____

c. _____

_____

4. Return with a gift

a. _____

_____

b. _____

_____

c. _____

_____

5. Serve others

a. _____

_____

b. _____

_____

c. _____

_____

PROBLEM SOLVING IN THREE STEPS

In many adventure races, I have served as the team navigator. That requires being able to check the map while running, so that we do not waste time. And it requires continually thinking about the big picture, where we are against my memory of the map. At a recent race, after 48 hours of travel, we jumped back on our bicycles for the last leg on paved roads. I began to sing Don McLean's "American Pie," and others joined in. We rode fast down from the mountains, along a river, in a single line called a pace-line, and thankful to be on the final stretch. We all sang louder. Then we came to an unfamiliar intersection. Huh? Where were we? I had lost my focus on the big picture mental map. Thankfully, there were roads and trails markers within sight. But we were off course, and my teammates were furious.

This problem-solving process has three steps. You can apply this process to any aspect of your future success.

STEP 1
Stop, take a breath, assess where you are, find some trail references.

STEP 2
Make a choice, create a map that focuses on the big picture..

STEP 3
Respond with useful feelings, words, and actions.

When our team was off course, I applied those three steps.

Step 1: We stopped and looked for clues. We quit singing. We looked for any landmark as a reference point and found a river, a bridge, three roads, some houses. Everyone shared whatever they saw. We focused on what we knew to be true, not what we thought could be true. The objective data in front of us defined our next steps.

Step 2: Next, we deduced that we were at a place where one road spun off along a river to the south. It was a dead end, as indicated by the road sign in front of us. Then we referred to our map. The objective data around us meant that there was only one place we could be, and we quickly discussed that information as a team. We then looked ahead to where we wanted to be, and determined the fastest way to get there. It required riding uphill and through a small town, some distractions. We shared the route plan and determined approximate time and distance. One person specialized as a time and distance monitor, using a bike odometer. Another person became more active as a second navigator. The fourth person was too emotionally disgusted to contribute to the team, but agreed to be quiet and follow the pace-line. Off we went.

Step 3: As the lead navigator, I was primarily responsible for our mistake. I knew that I had to respond to the team with useful feelings, words, and actions. After 48 hours of racing, we were pretty exhausted. I started with an apology and repeated that apology when it helped mollify a team member who could do little more than swear at me and the situation. I shared the map and started sentences with the objective facts. I changed my tone and used open-ended questions. For instance, "Well, we know that we were at this last checkpoint; then we traveled south along a river. Now we are someplace where three roads intersect and one is marked as a dead end. It seems logical to me that.... What do you think?" We continued on and finished the race in second place overall.

This three-step process will help you with your future success. You can apply it to problem solving, strategic planning, dealing with loved ones, or with that deadline ahead.

Here is another example. A friend of mine is an assistant headmaster of an independent high school. He recently described a situation that seemed like a "lose-lose" from all corners. The school had a tradition that seniors with a B or better grade point average were exempt from taking final examinations if they were in an advanced placement (AP) level course. Then in the fall, they decided to change the exam schedule so that exams were taken at the end of the second trimester, in April, before the AP's and scheduled trips abroad. The seniors and many parents revolted against the Head of School. They wanted exemptions and an earlier exam.

The administration felt trapped in a "lose-lose" dilemma pitting them against students and parents. Knowing that nothing could be further from the truth, the administration applied the three-step method above.

Step 1: They stopped the vicious rumors and scheduled a meeting that afternoon with the faculty, student leaders, and the senior administrators of the school.

Step 2: That group was charged with making a decision that would be shared with the community immediately afterwards on the website. Everyone knew that timetable. Everyone believed that a decision would, in fact, be made.

Step 3: Once a decision was proposed, the administration accepted it with one small adjustment and posted both the original proposal and their decision on the website. They invited concerned parents, students, and teachers to an open meeting the following afternoon. That prompt response included all constituents and reinforced that the administration was in charge.

Where do you need to apply this three-step process?

▲ ACTIVITY: USE THE THREE-STEP PROCESS

Directions: Use the following form, My Future Trails, to apply the three-step decision-making process to your life or work. Write or draw or speak your answers, and take notes along the way. Then review your notes. You may want to break these down into three separate sessions and include inquiries that promote reflection.

Step 1: Stop, take a breath, assess where you are, find some trail references. What can you stop doing that will give you some time to exhale? What are the objective facts around you? What is going well? What would you like to change?

Step 2: Make a choice, create a map that focuses on the big picture. What are several possible starting points? Select one that has passion for you. What would it look like if you acted in that way? What resources do you have for success? What resources do you need for success? What is the helicopter view from 10,000 feet on this adventure?

Step 3: Respond with useful feelings, words, and actions. How can you say or do what you need to? What can you implement right now? How would it feel to respond in that way?

The most successful personal maps start with your core values, are reviewed from a lofty perspective gained from the highest tree or ridgeline, and confirmed with fixed reference points.

When orienteering, that process is called triangulation. All you need are two confirmed reference points. For instance, if you can see a cell tower and the corner of a lake, you can take a compass bearing to each reference point. Where they intersect on the map is where you stand. You have made a map, you have selected some reference points, now you just need to apply that process to your goals.

Step 1: Stop, take a breath, assess where you are, find some trail references

_____
_____
_____
_____
_____
_____
_____

Step 2: Make a choice, create a map that focuses on the big picture

_____
_____
_____
_____
_____
_____

Step 3: Respond with useful feelings, words, and actions.

_____
_____
_____
_____
_____
_____

A LOFTY PERSPECTIVE

Imagine that you have a helicopter view on your world, from say 20,000 feet in the air. From that distance, you are able to look down upon the activities of a person who looks just like you, knows the same people, literally runs in the same circles. It could be you, except that you are 20,000 feet above that person. What do you observe from this lofty perspective?

You can only observe that other person's words and behavior. What they say defines them. What they do defines them. Any of their thoughts and feelings are buried under 20,000 feet of rushing air.

Most successful athletes use a lofty perspective to visualize success. Imagine being in a marathon and being 20,000 feet above the racers. As you look down on their bodies, you could focus on the leaders, or any individual. If the racer in the green shirt had distracting thoughts, you would not know them. Your lofty perspective forces you to focus only on words and behavior. That objective, distant perspective may help you, if you are the racer with a green shirt, to focus on your placement or the next challenge ahead.

The lofty perspective can be applied to any goal in your work or life. Imagine that you state that you will make five client calls each day, or spend more time listening to your partner. When you focus on the lofty perspective, you create enough distance that you can objectively study the data. How many client calls did you actually make? How many minutes did you spend actively listening to your partner?

Successful action often requires that helicopter perspective. A lofty perspective will help you be objective when studying your beliefs, words, actions, or any goal.

If you set your goal in the clouds, your attainment level will be higher than you might otherwise expect.

FINAL STORY

Many trainers have their versions of old stories, and here is one adapted from a coach and colleague, Deb Loucks.

There once was a curious person who was told that if he could stump the wise woman on the mountain he could learn anything he wanted. He was a restless person who had tried a number of careers and couldn't seem to settle down. He wanted answers to the core question, "What am I doing with my life?"

He did not know how to stump the wise woman on the mountain. But he did learn where she lived, hopped on a plane, and flew to the nearest city. He rented a car, and it was getting late. So he rented a hotel room. There he stood on the fourth floor balcony deck, watching the sun set. He was thinking about possible questions to stump the wise woman on the mountain. Nothing seemed satisfactory.

Suddenly a little bird flew nearby and slammed into the glass sliding door. It fell to the patio, temporarily knocked out. "Aha!" shouted our hero, "Now I know what to do!"

And so he reached down, scooped up the little bird into a towel, and locked it in his bathroom.

The next day, he packed his gear, wrapped up the little bird, and set off on his journey. He drove the rental car past towns, villages, and scattered houses; then finally parked at the trail head. He hefted his backpack, and gently carried the little bird, still wrapped in a towel. And so he hiked, for days on end. When the trail became steeper, he had to lean forward, sometimes balancing with a hand on the mountainside. Sometimes he placed the little bird inside his shirt while he struggled up and up, closer to the wise woman on the mountain.

Finally, he arrived at her cave. There he stood, with tattered clothes and a dirty face. He faced the woman, and she said, "You have come here with a gift wrapped in a towel; your desire is to stump me. Correct?"

"Yes," said the adventurer. "Here is my question. In my hands is a little bird. Is it alive or is it dead?"

Then he sat back with a bemused smile. He knew he had stumped her! If she said that the little bird was alive, then he could smash the little bird and show her the dead body. If she said the little bird was dead, then he could open the towel and let the bird fly away. He had stumped her, right?

The wise woman just laughed at him and quickly replied, "The answer is in your heart, the power is all in your hands."

Just like your future and this book. May you have a life filled with passionate action and many future trails!

Appendix 1:
Passionate Action
Assessment Inventory

As discussed in chapter six, there are four domains, four ways to look at creating extraordinary success in your life and work. These domains are based upon recent research in Multiple Intelligence, the different ways that we each interpret the world. Also, these domains are familiar to you. When you embrace your Passionate Action goals, you may notice these four domains – physical, emotional, cognitive, and spiritual aspects of your life. In chapter six, I explained how each of these four domains is a gift.

This self-assessment is designed to help you focus on your professional life and work, but it also can be applied to your personal life. For each of the statements listed below, circle the number that best indicates how you currently think or feel about yourself. There are no "right" or "wrong" answers; only your honest responses. Take about ten minutes.

		Not True	Slightly True	Mostly True	True
1	I am aware of the physical warning signs about my health.	1	2	3	4
2	At work, I know how my emotions impact my performance.	1	2	3	4
3	I know my strengths & limitations concerning my expertise at work.	1	2	3	4
4	I practice ways to tap into and nurture my spirit.	1	2	3	4
5	I am aware of the interplay between my mind, body, emotions, & spirit.	1	2	3	4
6	I get enough rest and sleep so that my energy is renewed.	1	2	3	4
7	I can bounce back after feeling disappointed.	1	2	3	4
8	When I express my values and beliefs, I try to do so in confident and constructive language that is neither aggressive nor defensive.	1	2	3	4
9	I know when I'm feeling whole or fragmented in how I'm living in the world.	1	2	3	4
10	I am aware of the impact of my self-talk on my emotions, body, & spirit.	1	2	3	4

		Not True	Slightly True	Mostly True	True
11	I am aware of how my physical presence affects my connection with my community and colleagues.	1	2	3	4
12	I am able to read other people's emotions from their affect and body language.	1	2	3	4
13	When noticing what others say and do, I assume best intentions.	1	2	3	4
14	I feel compassion for those struggling in life and recognize we are part of one mutually connected human community.	1	2	3	4
15	I follow the deeper wisdom of my body, mind, heart, and spirit to know what to do in emergency situations.	1	2	3	4
16	I mentor, coach, or intentionally contribute to developing others.	1	2	3	4
17	I regularly ask people about their emotional reactions to situations.	1	2	3	4
18	When in discussions with others I have the integrity and courage to maintain my beliefs even if they are unpopular.	1	2	3	4
19	When I could speak ill or well of another, I choose to speak well.	1	2	3	4
20	An integral part of my life involves speaking up for the dignity of those less fortunate and the balance and sustainability of nature.	1	2	3	4

Scoring Chart One: From the previous page, write into Scoring Chart #1 (below) your scores for each statement. Add the scores for each of the statements to determine your score for that domain. Use that number and the table in step two to determine your need for attention or change strategy. In the last two columns of your scoring chart, write whether there is a low, moderate, or high need for attention in that domain. Then write whether there is a need to reinforce, observe, or develop your change strategy.

Domain	Adding Scores	Score	Need for attention	Change Strategy
Physical Domain	1 ( ) + 6 ( ) + 11 ( ) + 16 ( ) =			
Emotional Domain	2 ( ) + 7 ( ) + 12 ( ) + 17 ( ) =			
Cognitive Domain	3 ( ) + 8 ( ) + 13 ( ) + 18 ( ) =			
Spiritual Domain	4 ( ) + 9 ( ) + 14 ( ) + 19 ( ) =			
Overall	5 ( ) + 10 ( ) + 15 ( ) + 20 ( ) =			

Domain Score	Need for Attention	Change Strategy
13+	Low	Reinforce
11-12	Moderate	Observe
Below 10	High	Develop

Hopefully you have just defined some areas with lower scores! These are areas with a "Moderate" or "High" need for attention. Not to worry – that is the value of any assessment inventory! To the extent that you were honest with yourself when you completed this assessment, it is a snapshot or a mirror of who you are right now.

Scoring Chart Two: From the previous page, write into Scoring Chart #2 (below) your scores for each statement. Once again, add the scores for each of the statements to determine your score for that quadrant. Use that number and the table to determine your need for attention or change strategy.

Domain	Adding Scores	Score	Need for attention	Change Strategy
Self Awareness	1 ( ) + 2 ( ) + 3 ( ) + 4 ( ) + 5 ( ) =			
Self Care	6 ( ) + 7 ( ) + 8 ( ) + 9 ( ) + 10 ( )=			
Social Awareness	11 ( ) + 12 ( ) + 13 ( ) + 14 ( ) + 15 ( ) =			
Social Contribution	16 ( ) + 17 ( ) + 18 ( ) + 19 ( ) + 20 ( ) =			

Domain Score	Need for Attention	Change Strategy
17+	Low	Reinforce
14-16	Moderate	Observe
Below 13	High	Develop

YOUR PASSIONATE ACTION QUADRANTS

	SELF	OTHERS
AWARENESS	SELF AWARENESS	SOCIAL AWARENESS
ACTIONS	SELF CARE	SOCIAL CONTRIBUTION

THE PASSIONATE ACTION QUADRANTS

You may be wondering about the four quadrants described in step three. As described in chapter six, this four-quadrant model is a simple way to look at any domain of passionate action. You can apply these four quadrants to any domain, whether physical, emotional, cognitive, or spiritual. The left side of the quadrant looks at your individual experience; the right side looks at your experience with others. The top half of the quadrant looks at your awareness of passionate action; the bottom half looks at your actions. Think of this four-quadrant model as four ways to apply the Passionate Action Model.

So, how do you develop skills or competencies in any of these areas? Start by circling those areas in chart two that indicate a moderate or high need for attention. Your Passionate Action goal may be to develop some aspect of yourself in any of those areas. Thankfully, there are many ways to learn or develop skills. Here are 16 examples, to get you started. I am confident that you can add some practices of your own. Use these 16 sample practices to develop specific competencies toward your Passionate Action goals.

PHYSICAL DOMAIN PRACTICES

Self Awareness: Notice where you hold stress or tension in your body – such as your jaw, stomach, neck, back, or so forth. Pay attention to your breathing, right now – is it shallow or deep? Notice when you find yourself holding your breath, and when you breathe in a smooth, continuous way.

Self Care: For one week, eat nutritious and healthful foods, have caffeine or sugar in minimal amounts, walk or exercise 30 minutes daily, and get a good night's sleep every night. Journal what results from these practices.

Social Awareness: Notice what messages you get from the way

others present themselves physically. Watch their body language. Notice how others use their body to express who they are.

Social Contribution: Experiment with different ways that you can physically express yourself in conversation. Offer to help strangers. Model openness and accessibility to others. Ask a coach to observe you, then provide feedback on your contributions to others.

EMOTIONAL DOMAIN PRACTICES

Self Awareness: Notice when your emotions shift throughout the day. As accurately as possible, notice when you are feeling happy, sad, angry, or fearful. Notice what triggers those emotions.

Self Care: When you are angry, recognize that you are in that emotion. Practice pausing for at least ten seconds, or until the anger passes. Then consider several options for expressing yourself. Say or do less than you feel. Use the Communication Wheel in chapter six

Social Awareness: Enter several groups during the day. Notice the emotional impact that others have one another in each of those groups. Notice how you feel in each of those groups. Notice how their emotions affect yours.

Social Contribution: When someone you know is suffering (with sadness, anger, or fear), notice the impact on their well-being when you are with them. State that you care, in a non-judgmental and compassionate way. Listen for five seconds before replying. Avoid trying to fix anyone or make things better.

COGNITIVE DOMAIN PRACTICES

Self Awareness: Notice your internal dialogue when you think about your day or your life. Is your self-language critical or appreciative or something else? Notice how your self-talk impacts your attitude.

Self Care: When you think others do not like you, speak your views calmly and clearly. Practice doing so in private, then in public – even if you think you may stutter. Then ask yourself, how did speaking calmly and clearly affect your thoughts about intellectual integrity?

Social Awareness: Study several groups. Notice the different responses from people in positions of authority when they speak to others in a well-reasoned manner. Take notes about the process – what you think is going on in the meeting. Notice how reason and logic contribute to each group.

Social Contribution: Speak up in any conversation. If you think someone sounds disrespectful of another person or group, speak up and ask if that was their intention. Let it be known that you are standing witness to the dignity of others. Notice how your actions make a difference in the behavior of others, and in the integrity of the conversation.

SPIRITUAL DOMAIN PRACTICES

Self Awareness: Notice when you experience a sense of connection and flow with life. Reflect upon or pray for whatever you are grateful about in your life. Make a list and add to it for two weeks. Read that list every morning for the following week.

Self Care: Take 20 minutes each day to do something that makes you feel more harmonious with life. Give yourself a gift – whether through yoga, art, music, dance, physical activity, being in nature, meditating, volunteering to serve others, or some other avenue. Enjoy those 20 minutes!

Social Awareness: Notice what kinds of activities build a sense of esprit de corps in your groups or organizations. Observe how kindness affects the energy or creative power of the people involved.

Social Contribution: In group discussions, experiment with introducing a topic that is important to the well-being of the world community (e.g., international conflict, diversity, AIDS, pollution, and so forth). Speak carefully. Model mutual respect and allow insights for learning. Help others learn to listen and inquire. Then journal about your experience.

Appendix 2:
Exercises from
This Book

APPENDIX II:
EXERCISES FROM THIS BOOK

CHAPTER 3 – GET THE MESSAGE

- Time slices. Compare and contrast 24 hourly slices from your actual day and your ideal day.

- My place of power. Imagine that place, then draw or write it so that you create a tangible reminder.

- Think it and ink it. Complete a timeline for each decade of your life. Also, list 101 of your life goals, then sort them based on possible Passionate Action goals.

- Divine messages. Sit alone in silence and call forth a divine form with a message for you.

- Future self. Listen to this guided meditation and record the name, appearance, advice, and gift from your future self.

- Assessment inventories. Do the Passionate Action Assessment Inventory in the appendix.

■ Action items. See the list of possibilities. Self-coaching and reflective questions are throughout the chapter.

CHAPTER 4 – LEAVE THE FAMILIAR

■ Take a visit. Follow these four messages to see where they lead.

■ The balance wheel. Using the categories provided, or some others, determine how balanced your wheel of life is. Compare and contrast your current reality with your ideal life.

■ Risk taking and risk avoidance. Complete the risk scales and apply to the familiar aspects of your life.

■ Baseline tables. Using the sample provided, complete your baseline table for familiar aspects of your life.

■ Action plans. Select a Passionate Action goal. Then complete one of the two sample action plans for that goal.

■ Quadrant models. Complete the sample quadrants for motivation and time management.

■ Action items. See the list of possibilities.

■ Self-coaching and reflective questions are throughout the chapter.

CHAPTER 5 – CONFRONT CHALLENGES

■ The action learning model. Apply these four points to your Passionate Action goal.

■ Pleasure/pain motivators. Use the sample to determine your motivators for change.

■ The G R O W model. Use the model and self-coaching questions to confront the essential challenges in your life.

■ Let's make a movie. Have fun imagining yourself as the star in an action movie, then play out that role.

■ Shackleton's story. Use his incredible adventure as a backdrop to explore your challenges and responses.

■ Learn from our mistakes. Using the examples and questions, note significant mistakes in your life.

■ Action items. See the list of possibilities.

■ Self-coaching and reflective questions are throughout the chapter.

CHAPTER 6 – RETURN WITH A GIFT

■ Physical gifts. Use the quadrant model and assessment inventory in the appendix to determine your physical gifts.

■ The communication wheel. Adopt this model, practice using these five steps, and notice how it affects yourself and others.

■ Emotional gifts. Use the quadrant model and assessment inventory in the appendix to determine your emotional gifts.

■ Cognitive gifts. Use the quadrant model and assessment inventory in the appendix to determine your cognitive gifts.

■ Signature strengths. Identify the core signature strengths that are important to you and apply them to your life.

■ Spiritual gifts. Use the quadrant model and assessment inventory in the appendix to determine your spiritual gifts.

■ Action items. See the list of possibilities.

■ Self-coaching and reflective questions are throughout the chapter.

CHAPTER 7 – SERVE OTHERS

■ Sacred acts. Identify the sacred acts in your life and determine how they help to serve others.

■ Daily power questions. Adopt these into your daily ritual and notice the results.

■ Creating your service business. Complete the charts to determine your marketing niche, business strategy, and unique service niche.

■ The adventure of parenting. Use the series of questions, or modify them for your adventure goal.

■ Action items. See the list of possibilities.

■ Self-coaching and reflective questions are throughout the chapter.

Recommended Reading

Anderson, Merrill. *Executive Briefing: Case Study on the Return on Investment of Executive Coaching.* MetrixGlobal, LLC, 2001.

Armstrong, Lance and Chris Carmichael. *The Lance Armstrong Performance Program: The Training, Strengthening, and Eating Plan Behind the World's Greatest Cycling Victory.* Rodale Books, 2000.

Blanchard, Ken. *The One Minute Manager Balances Work and Life: A Healthy Lifestyle Is the Key to Success.* New York: William Morrow & Co, 1986.

Buzan, Tony. *The Mind Map Book: How to Use Radiant Thinking to Maximize Your Brain's Untapped Potential.* New York: Dutton, 1993.

Bridges, William. *Managing Transition: Making the Most of Change.* Cambridge, MA: Perseus Books, 2003.

Campbell, Joseph. *The Hero with a Thousand Faces.* Princeton, NJ: Princeton University Press, 1972.

Campbell, Joseph with Bill Moyers. *The Power of Myth.* New York: Doubleday, 1988.

Carmichael, Chris. *The Ultimate Ride: Get Fit, Get Fast and Start Winning with the World's Top Cycling Coach.* New York: G.P. Putnam's Sons, 2003.

Carson, Rick. *Taming the Gremlin: A Guide to Enjoying Yourself.* New York: Perennial (HarperCollins), 1990.

Covey, Stephen. *The Seven Habits of Highly Effective People: Restoring the Character Ethic.* New York: Simon and Schuster, 1989.

Csikszentmihalyi, Mihaly. *Flow: The Psychology of Optimal Experience.* New York: Harper & Row, 1990.

Dotlich, David, and Peter Cairo. *Action Coaching: How to Leverage Individual Performance for Company Success.* San Francisco: Jossey-Bass Publishers, 1999.

Frankl, Victor. *Man's Search for Ultimate Meaning.* New York: Perseus Publishing, 2000.

Goleman, Daniel. *Emotional Intelligence: Why it Can Matter More Than IQ.* New York: Bantam, 1995.

Goleman, Daniel. *Working with Emotional Intelligence.* New York: Bantam, 1998.

Greenleaf, Robert. *Servant Leadership: A Journey into the Nature of Legitimate Power and Greatness.* New York: Paulist Press, 1991.

Hammond, Sue. *The Thin Book of Appreciative Inquiry.* Plano, TX: Kodiak Consulting, 1996.

His Holiness the Dalai Lama and Howard Cutler. *The Art of Happiness at Work.* New York: Riverhead/Penguin Books, 2003.

Kimbro, Dennis. *What Makes the Great Great: Strategies for Extraordinary Achievement.* New York: Doubleday, 1998.

Kiyosaki, Robert and Sharon Lechter. *Rich Dad, Poor Dad: What the Rich Teach their Kids About Money – That the Poor and Middle Class Do Not!* New York: Warner Books, 2000.

Perkins, Dennis. *Leading at the Edge: Leadership Lessons from the Extraordinary Saga of Shackleton's Antarctic Expedition.* New York, Amacom, 2000.

Robbins, Anthony. *Awaken the Giant Within: How to Take Immediate Control of Your Mental, Emotional, Physical, and Financial Destiny!* New York: Simon and Schuster, 1991.

Salz, Jeff. *The Way of Adventure: Transforming Your Life and Work with Spirit and Vision.* New York: John Wiley & Sons, 2000.

Seligman, Martin. *Authentic Happiness: Using the New Positive Psychology to Realize your Potential for Lasting Fulfillment.* New York: Free Press, 2002.

Seligman, Martin. *Learned Optimism: How to Change Your Mind and Your Life.* New York: Simon and Schuster, 1998.

Seligman, Martin. *The Optimistic Child: Proven Program to Safeguard Children from Depression and Build Lifelong Resistance.* New York: Harper Collins, 1995.

Senge, Peter, Art Kleiner, Charlotte Roberts, Richard Ross, and Bryan Smith. *The Fifth Discipline Handbook: Strategies and Tools for Building a Learning Organization.* New York: Doubleday, 1994.

Silberkeit, David. *A New Adventure Every Day: 541 Simple Ways to Live with Pizzazz.* Naperville, IL: Sourcebooks, 2002.

Sleamaker, Rob and Ray Browning. *SERIOUS Training for Endurance Athletes.* Champaign, IL: Human Kinetics, 1996.

Smith, Benson and Tony Rutigliano. *Discover Your Sales Strengths; How the World's Greatest Salespeople Develop Winning Careers.* New York: Warner Business Books, 2003.

Steinbeck, John. Travels with Charley: *In Search of America.* New York: Viking Press, 1962.

Warren, Rick. *The Purpose-Driven Life: What on Earth Am I Here For?* Grand Rapids, MI: Zondervan, 2002.

Whitmore, John. *Coaching for Performance; Growing People, Performance and Purpose.* 3rd edition. London: Nicholas Brealey, 2003.

Whitworth, Laura, Henry Kimsey-House, and Phil Sandahl. *Co-Active Coaching: New Skills for Coaching People toward Success in Work and Life.* Palo Alto, CA: Davies-Black Publishing, 1998.

Wilson, Larry and Hersch Wilson. *Play to Win: Choosing Growth Over Fear in Work and Life.* Austin, TX: Bard Press, 1998.

Wycoff, Joyce. *Mindmapping: Your Personal Guide to Exploring Creativity and Problem-Solving.* New York: Berkley, 1991.

Zimmerman, Alan. *Brave Questions: Building Stronger Relationships by Asking All the Right Questions.* Prior Lake, MN: Zimmerman Communi-Care Network, Inc, 2003.

NOTES

NOTES

NOTES

NOTES

NOTES

NOTES

COACHING, SPEAKING, AND TRAINING

Doug Gray, PCC, or an associate would be delighted to work with your group or organization. We guarantee an interactive, entertaining, useful training or event!

Coaching
Individual, Group, Organizational

Speaking titles include:
Creating Action-based Success
Extreme Productivity
Building Your Winning Team
Creating Customer Delight
Connection Marketing
Achieving Your Business Goals

Training Seminars include the above and:
Managing Interpersonal Relationships,
or Emotional Intelligence 101
Coaching 101: How to Use Coaching to Grow Your Business
The 12 Foundations of Leadership
Leadership Training for Your Team
Coaching for Increased Sales
Change Management

For availability and details, contact
www.action-learning.com
doug@action-learning.com
or 704.895.6479

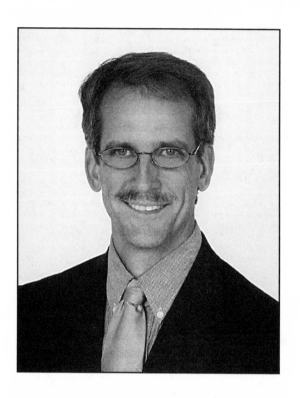

Doug Gray, PCC, an ICF-certified coach, speaker and leadership trainer, founded Action Learning Associates, Inc. in 1997. The company's clients range from small business owners to Fortune 50 corporations. Doug holds a MALS degree from Dartmouth College. He co-developed the Leadership Development Institute at the University of Maryland and has taught there since 2000. He is an adjunct faculty member at North Carolina State University. Doug is an extreme athlete who loves competitive adventure (endurance) racing. He lives with his wife and children in North Carolina.

Action Learning Associates designs and facilitates individual, executive, and team experiential learning programs. To learn more about Action Learning Associates' coaching programs, team building and leadership development, visit www.action-learning.com or email Doug Gray at doug@action-learning.com.